GERMAN AND AUSTRIAN AVIATION OF WORLD WAR I

A PICTORIAL CHRONICLE OF THE AIRMEN AND
AIRCRAFT THAT FORGED GERMAN AIRPOWER

MW01000259

AVIATION PIONEERS

GERMAN AND AUSTRIAN AVIATION OF WORLD WAR I

A PICTORIAL CHRONICLE OF THE AIRMEN AND AIRCRAFT THAT FORGED GERMAN AIRPOWER

HUGH W. COWIN

First published in Great Britain in 2000 by Osprey Publishing
Elms Court, Chapel Way, Botley, Oxford OX2 9LP, UK
Email: info@ospreypublishing.com

ISBN 1 84176 069 2

Editor: Shaun Barrington
Design: The Black Spot
Origination: Grasmere Digital Imaging, Leeds, UK
Printed in Hong Kong through Worldprint Ltd

00 01 02 03 04   10 9 8 7 6 5 4 3 2 1

For a catalogue of all books published by Osprey Military, Automotive and Aviation please write to:

The Marketing Manager, Osprey Direct, PO Box 140, Wellingborough, Northants, NN8 4ZA, United Kingdom E-mail: info@ospreydirect.co.uk

Visit Osprey's website at: www.ospreypublishing.com

Existing and forthcoming books in the Aviation Pioneers series:

Acknowledgements

I am, as usual, indebted to a small band of loyal supporters who have provided both moral and material support to sustain me while producing this work: they are Norman R. Bartlett, Andy Bunce of British Aerospace Systems, John Edwards and Peter Elliott of the RAF Museum, Ray Funnell, Mike Hooks, Philip Jarrett, Teddy Nevill of TRH Pictures and Andrew Siddons of Rolls-Royce. A very large vote of thanks must also go to the many unknown and unsung German and Austrian World War I photographers, both military and civilian, without whose images this book would have needed far more words than it has. Wherever possible picture sources are identified in brackets at the end of the caption.

Front cover, above left Rumpler C I. *Below left* Friedrichshafen G III. *Right* Friedrich Ritter von Roth. (All Cowin Collection). *Rear cover* Junkers CI I. (Junkers).

Hugh W. Cowin was born in January 1934 and spent 12 years in the RAF between 1951 and 1963, mainly with all-weather fighter units. His last five and a half years were spent with the Central Fighter Establishment at RAF West Raynham. He then went into the aerospace industry, culminating in his setting up and heading the Central Market and Research Department for what was to become Lucas Aerospace. A consultant to Fairey Hydraulics since 1972, he retained his pilot's licence and ratings until October 1979. Along the way, he has found time to found *Flight International's* Systems feature, produce the Observer's *Warships* and collect aircraft photographs. Hugh Cowin has also written the first two volumes in this series: Aviation Pioneers 1: *Research Aircraft 1891-1970: X-Planes;* and **Aviation Pioneers 2:** *Racing & Record Setting Aircraft - The Risk Takers.*

Contents

(Frontispiece) Propaganda, at its simplest the art of deriding your enemies while bolstering your own image, had emerged long before World War I, but could be said to have gained new strength during the conflict. For example, this photograph of **Baron Manfred von Richthofen**, Germany`s highest scoring fighter ace with 80 confirmed victories, seen here standing with the German Empress in May 1917, was not taken at the personal whim of either, but was part of a calculated propaganda campaign built around the man. Already exalted by the military publicists as the steely-eyed, inveterate killer of the skies to his colleagues fighting in the air alongside him and in the trenches below, Manfred von Richthofen needed an altogether gentler image for consumption by German womenfolk at home, hence this particular picture. The Red Baron, as publicists dubbed him, was far from alone in being given such treatment, other fighter aces' efforts being equally heralded. A fighter pilot's effectiveness was of course far more easily measured – and trumpeted – than the complex teamwork required of a reconnaissance machine's crew. Thus, despite the fact that the work of the 'recce' fliers was of paramount value and probably called for a higher sustained level of courage overall, the fighter pilot, with his highly visible victory score, stole the glory. In contrast, the unsung 'recce' crews were routinely asked to fly ever more hours in slower, less agile aircraft than fighters and besides doing their own demanding task, would often have to fight their way out and back against the concerted efforts of the enemy's fighters. (Cowin Collection)

Preface

Aviation had come a long way in a technical sense during the few short years between the Wright Brothers's first powered flight of 17 December 1903 and the outbreak of World War I on 3 August 1914, but was still very much in its infancy in industrial terms. The war changed that state of affairs very quickly. With the onset of war, aviation became a tool of the military, who, seeing its potential as an 'eye in the sky', gave what had been little more than a cottage industry not just a sense of focus, but, by previous standards, vast injections of cash. Thus, the business of designing and building aircraft was, within the span of less than two years, transformed into a substantial industry in its own right.

However, the military, having taken effective control of the industry, did far more than simply inject cash, they infused the business of aircraft manufacture with a sense of direction and discipline, from which flowed such useful

practices as methodical crash investigation and the whole culture of flight safety as applicable to both design and operations. Meanwhile, as the war progressed, the military was, itself, learning and becoming more organised and, in the process, discovering an ever broader range of requirements for which aircraft could be adopted. To cite two important examples, while the Italians had dropped the first bomb from an aeroplane as early as 1911, the problems of organised aerial bombing were only addressed once war was declared. Similarly, while a number of nations had experimented with fitting guns to aircraft prior to the war, the emergence of the dedicated fighter aircraft only really came about in the early months of 1915, as a counter to the highly effective intrusiveness of enemy reconnaissance overflights.

The military suffered the occasional setback as they stumbled along the learning curve of just how to employ aircraft. This was particularly so in Germany where the pre-war

efforts of Graf von Zeppelin and the sheer scale of his airships had seemingly made an indelible impact on the German national psyche. As it transpired, the Zeppelin and other makes of military airship never lived up to their inital promise and although the German Imperial Navy resolutely clung to operating airships throughout the war, the German Army harboured few illusions concerning airship vulnerability and abandoned their use long before the Armistice.

While the impact of World War I on the development of the aircraft industries within many nations was of overall massive benefit in terms of growth, both physically and financially, the same could hardly be said when it came to evolving the aircraft technically. Indeed, recalling the grace and speed achieved by such aircraft as the 1913 Deperdussin racing monoplane, the first two years of war saw many seemingly retrogressive developments. The elegant monoplanes of the immediate pre-war years largely gave way to the biplane, whose undoubtedly more robust, box-structure double wing form found favour with the cautious military mind. During this period the emphasis switched from speed to load-carrying capability

as aeroplanes were crammed with cameras, guns or bombs, causing typical top speeds to drop off at a faster rate than they had progressed in the two years prior to war! This innate military conservatism towards the fundamental development of aircraft is, at least in part, explained by the ever-present pressures to produce quantitavely more of the same, rather than fewer, or the same amount, of something better. This apparent apathy on the part of the military towards pushing the boundaries of aircraft design, it should be noted, was just as manifest in France, which at the outset of the war was the most technologically advanced of all the aircraft producing nations, as it was among the more laggardly countries. This said, it is interesting to note that when an aircraft builder, such as Hugo Junkers or Claudius Dornier came up with a really radical design, it was seldom dismissed out of hand. This was particularly true of the German Army, who, regardless of their reputation for 'doing things by the book` provided Junkers with the necessary financial support over an extended period, at a time when each new design from his drawing boards appeared to be a worse performer than his last.

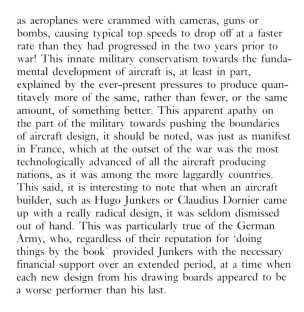

Typical of the two seat reconnaissance biplanes in service with the German Imperial Air Service at the outbreak of war was this **Gotha B**. First flown at the start of 1914, the LD-1a became the B on entering military service, signifying it to be the first biplane type purchased from the firm. Had it been a monoplane, it would have carried the military designation Gotha A, with subsequent types becoming Gotha A 2s or B 2s, etc. Powered by a 100hp Daimler D I, the prototype was followed by ten further examples, 458/14 to 467/14, these machines differing from the first in being fitted with a 100hp Oberursal copy of the original Gnome Monosoupape, as seen here. The Gotha B's top level speed was 71.5mph, while its maximum range was 323 miles. (Cowin Collection)

Preparations

On 3 August 1914, Germany, along with the Austro-Hungarian Empire, collectively known as the Central Powers, declared war upon France. On the following day, Britain was drawn in thanks to its treaty obligations to Belgium, as that country was trampled by German invaders. Thus, within a matter of hours, Europe had become embroiled in a conflict that was to grow into one of unprecedented scale and intensity, a war in which millions were to die. It was also the first war ever, thanks to aviation, where the fighting and its associated destruction could be visited on civilian populations sometimes well over a hundred miles from the front lines, let alone the air bases from which the bombers departed and returned.

Military aviation in early August 1914 was still very much in its infancy with only a few nations having anything resembling a coherent air force. Of this handful of nations Germany had the largest number of operationally deployed aircraft, with 258, excluding kite balloons and a handful of airships, the majority of which were sited on the Western Front. Facing the Germans, France and Britain could only muster 156 and 63 heavier-than-air machines respectively, at the front. Further, it is generally acknowledged that, at this time, the German forces were better organised. It should be emphasised that these remarks apply to the German Imperial Army Air Service, as opposed to the German Imperial Naval Air Service, which was not only much smaller, but at this time was centred around a largely still to be furnished airship fleet as its primary asset, the aeroplane seen as very secondary in terms of operational importance. Of the other initial belligerent nations, only the Austro-Hungarians had a tiny, but reasonably organised army air arm equipped with land-based aircraft, while the Hungarian Navy largely operated small flying boats. Generally, these machines were of Austrian design and manufacture and were of fairly mediocre capability. The one exception were the Lohner flying boats, that were widely copied or licensed in Italy, France and Germany. From all surviving documentation, what Russian military aviation there was at the outset of World War I was both pitifully scant and unorganised.

So much for quantitative analysis. Here, it is pertinent to make a qualitative assessment. At this time, virtually all of the world's air arms operated a motley assortment of aircraft types and such developments as type and even role standardisation were some way off. Perhaps the only meaningful yardstick to apply in assessing an air arm was the size of its flight training effort. In this, only France and Germany are worthy of consideration, with Germany just edging ahead in the annual numbers of pilots and observers produced. The real build-up in German military heavier-than-air aviation commenced in 1911, 37 machines bought by year-end. During 1912, emphasis was given to the training of pilots and observers, the army's limited facilities augmented by the contracting of civilian flying schools, mainly off-shoots of the aircraft manufacturers, to meet the planned growth in throughput.

Below The **Etriche Taube** two seater of Austrian origin first flew in November 1909 and was adopted by the German military in 1911 as their standard reconaissance and training type. Most were built under licence in Germany by Rumpler. They were withdrawn from front line service by mid-1915. This is a 1912 Taube fitted with a 100hp Daimler D.I. giving a top level speed of 71mph. (*Cowin Collection*)

Above right **Anthony Fokker**, pilot and aircraft manufacturer, had the entrepreneur's innate gift for getting it right in his business decisions. An early example of this was his setting up of the Fokker Flying School at Doberitz, close to Berlin in late 1912. When the German Army announced their plan to sub-contract flying training to civilian organisations in 1912, Fokker grasped the opportunity of establishing close personal contact with the the future leaders of German military aviation. Although Fokker left the day-to-day training chores to his flying instructors, he was the school's Chief Flying Instructor and Examiner. Fokker is seen here sitting on the axle of one of his Fokker Spin two seaters, amid one of his early military intakes. (*Cowin Collection*)

Stahl-Eindecker Roland Typ 1914
der Luft-Fahrzeug-Gesellschaft Johannisthal

Above One of the so-called **Steel Taubes**, built by **LFG Roland** during 1914. Employing a steel tube structure in place of the Etrich's original wooden one, the 100hp Daimler having now become a 100hp Mercedes D I. Despite these changes, performance, or at least the 71mph top level speed appears to have changed little. Note the retention of wing warping and the distance between pilot in the rear and the front seated observer, something that could not have helped in-flight communications. (Cowin Collection)

Below The **Albatros WMZ** of 1911 was generally considered to be the German Imperial Naval Air Service's first practical seaplane, but aeroplanes were to take a back seat to airships in pre-war naval plans. (Cowin Collection)

Above right The Gotha LE-3, military designation Gotha A I of 1914, was yet another minor variation on the Etrich Taube theme. Gotha built 20 of these two seaters with the army serials A79/14 to A91/14, A119/14 to A125 and A137/14 to A142/14. Employing the 100hp Mercedes D I, range for the machine was quoted as 239 miles. (Cowin Collection)

Bottom This Pfalz-built **Otto Biplane**, seen here in happier, pre-war times, was the only aircraft available in German East Africa at the outbreak of war and as such was pressed into military service, along with its pilot, Bruno Buckner. (Cowin Collection)

Opposite, top First flown in early 1914, this Albatros two seater, along with a slightly smaller version, was adopted by the army as the **Albatros B I** and **B II**, respectively. Between them, these two unarmed machines provided most of German aerial reconnaissance capability well into 1915. Thanks to their relatively viceless handling characteristics, both the B I and B II stayed in production, albeit relegated to the training role, into

1917. Power for both aircraft was either a 100hp Mercedes, or a 110hp Benz Bz I, giving the pair a top level speed of around 65mph at sea level. (Cowin Collection)

Below Little valid information survives on this Austrian Army Air Service-operated Lloyd C I of early 1914 design origins, other than that it was powered by a 120hp Austro-Daimler and that it set a new altitude record of 21,709 feet on 27 June 1914. Only built in small numbers, the type led to the Lloyd C II through C V series, the workhorses of both the reconnaissance and training units of the Austro-Hungarian Air Service; reconnaissance, in the early years, being the only real function of military aircraft. (Cowin Collection)

The Lofty Overview

Although the value of aviation as a reconnaissance tool had initially been established by the German Army during its annual exercise of June 1911, its use remained confined to providing post-flight situation reports made to Corps, or Army-level Headquarter staff. For operational purposes, the aeroplane, with its relatively modest radius of action, was to undertake tactical reconnaissance, while the longer ranged airships would carry out strategic reconnaissance. This state of affairs was to remain essentially unaltered through to the outset of war. This mode of operating clearly had its limitations, prime among which was that the value of tactical information, such as train movement sightings, is a perishable commodity and becomes less useful the longer the time delay between sighting and reporting. Thus, at the outset of war, this perishability factor worked against the best efforts of the 33 deployed Field Flying Sections, or Feldflieger Abteilungen, each of which was equipped with six A (unarmed monoplane) or B (unarmed biplane) two seaters, because of the highly mobile nature of the battle lines during most of the first month. However, once the fighting had settled into its essentially static mode by the beginning of September 1914, then the value of the reconnaissance aeroplane rapidly came to the fore. This should be contrasted with the abysmal failure of the airship in operations, with four lost during the first month of the war, a setback that led directly to the army confining its airship fleet to night-only operations from then on. This limitation on the inherently low speed airship was extremely severe, curtailing its one major advantage over the aeroplane, that of range. In contrast, the German Navy's airships, used for both reconnaissance and bombing, survived their initial operational deployment better and with fewer losses, but, of course, these craft were largely operating over the vast expanses of the Baltic and North Sea far removed from enemy defences and where they had room to better weather-out the unanticipated storm.

With the early onset of the largely static trench warfare that so characterised World War I, the Germans were quick to realise another role in which the two seat aeroplane could be employed, namely that of close air support for their infantry. In these missions, the machine's observer was used to harass the enemy's front lines by rifle fire and dropping light bombs, the latter being done fairly haphazardly at first while awaiting the development of an effective aiming method. Such was the clamour from the ground troops for close air support, that a further requirement soon arose for a specially dedicated ground attack machine, the Cl class aircraft, with their armour cladding aimed at reducing vunerability to ground fire. In parallel with these close air support tasks, the Field Flying Sections were, thanks to advances in airborne radio telephony, beginning to undertake another important function, that of directing fire and spotting fall of shell for the artillery. The possible doubts about the value of the 'eye in the sky' that may have been voiced during the first weeks of the war had long since vanished, the two seaters were here to stay.

Thus, by the summer of 1915, the modestly performing two seaters with which the army entered the war had evolved into the more powerful and armed C class machines, capable of undertaking a variety of offensive and defensive tasks at both high and low levels. Such had been the efficacy of the aeroplane in providing invaluable tactical information to the commanders in the field that, as early as the close of 1914, the French in particular were being driven to produce a gun-carrying counter to these ever-probing German aerial incursions.

Left An admirable air-to-air image of a **Rumpler** 5A, military designation **C I**, an armed and more powerful derivative of the company's B I. First flown towards the end of 1914, the Rumpler C I was powered by a 160hp Mercedes D III, giving it a top level speed of 94mph at sea level. The C I's handling docility was matched by what was, for its time, an impressive high altitude ability, the operational ceiling being quoted as 16,600 feet. This translates into the machine being able to overfly enemy territory largely immune from interception unless caught by an enemy standing patrol already at or above its own altitude. For defence at lower altitudes, the C I's rear seated observer was equipped with a flexibly-mounted 7.92mm Parabellum gun, later added to by providing the pilot with a fixed, forward firing 7.92mm Spandau, useful for trench strafing, on the C Ia. Although the actual production figures have not survived, the C I was known to have been built in sustantial numbers by Rumpler and four sub-contractors, with around 250 serving in operational units in October 1916. Allowing for attrition and other factors, it would be safe to assume total C I build to be well in excess of 500 machines. The C I pictured here belonged to the Schleissheim-based advanced flight training unit tasked with bringing trainee crews up to full operational standard. (Cowin Collection)

Bottom The **Albatros B I** typified the fragility of the early reconnaissance machines fielded by the armies on both sides of the line and on all fronts. Nonetheless, the vital importance of these machines was to be displayed for the all world to see during the five-day Battle of Tannenberg that commenced on 26 August 1914, during which the Russians were rebuffed, with the loss of 30,000 dead and 90,000 captured.

Although initially designed as a high performance two seater, the **Gotha LD-5** was rejected for field service as other than a single seat advanced trainer and even in this role, its small wing area and consequent high wing loading would ensure that it was confined to operating from the longest of available airstrips. First flown in December 1914, the LD-5 used a 100hp Oberursel Ur I, but no other useful performance data survives. The real mystery surrounding the LD-5, however, is how Gotha were permitted to build no less than 13 of these fairly pilot-unfriendly looking brutes. (Cowin Collection)

Opposite, top This unarmed **Aviatik B II**, serial 34.08, was built by the Austrian-based branch of the company for service with the Austro-Hungarian forces, powered by a 100hp Mercedes. Of late 1914 origins, only a relatively small number of B IIs were produced, the type being quickly superseded by the more powerful, cleaner and armed Aviatik C I. As was often the case, once relegated from front-line service, the type found a second career with advanced flying training units, the Aviatik B II known to have served in this role with FEA 9 at Darmstadt during 1916. (Cowin Collection)

Below Only ten of these 1915 two seat **Gotha B Is** were produced, just suffcent to equip a single Field Flight Section, although no evidence of their deployment, if ever, has survived. Using a 120hp Mercedes D Ia, the LD-7 to give its design bureau designation, had a top level speed of 77.5mph, with a range of 330 miles. (Cowin Collection)

Above, right This **Albatros C I** observer demonstrates just how crude manual bomb dropping could be in the late spring of 1915. The weapon he is posing with is the standard 10 Kg/22lb high explosive bomb introduced the previous year. By mid-1916, such weapons would be fitted to remotely released, underwing bomb racks for providing close air support to the infantry. (Cowin Collection)

Right The **Albatros C I**, deployed operationally from the spring of 1915, soon built a reputation for its ease of handling and general robustness. During its two year production life, the C I

underwent a series of changes, being fitted with ever more powerful engines starting with the 150hp Benz Bz III and ending with the 180hp Argus As III. Along with these changes of engine, the position of the radiator moved around, starting on the fuselage flank in the C I, but moving to drape from the upper wing's

centre section leading edge, as here on this C Ia. Top level speed of the C Ia was 87mph at sea level, with a ceiling of 9,840 feet. The armament comprised a single, flexibly-mounted 7.92mm Parabellum in the rear cockpit. (Cowin Collection)

Oops! The **Albatros C I** of Lt Maass, Fl Abt 14, after nosing over in the snow at Subat on the Eastern Front during January 1916. The standard practice appears to have been that any new type found its way, initially, to the Western Front, then the Eastern Front, where the opposition was likely to be less fierce. Finally, when considered operationally obsolete, the machine would frequently pass into the training role. (Cowin Collection)

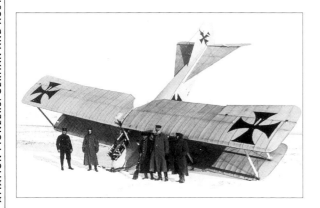

Lohner of Austria, besides producing their admirable line of small, agile flying boats, also built a series of land-based, reconnaissance two-seaters for the Austro-Hungarian Air Service. In

stark contrast to their flying boats, these B and C class designs, spanning the years 1913 to 1917, proved mediocre performers and, in consequence, each variant was only built in small numbers. The 1915 **Lohner B.VII,** 17.00, seen here, despite its 160hp Austro-Daimler, could only achieve a top level speed of 85 mph at sea level. As in this case, despite their B class designations, many two seaters were retrospectively fitted with a gun in the rear seat, thus converting them, effectively, into C types. (Cowin Collection)

Below The intriguing twin-boom fuselaged **Ago C II** of late summer 1915 origins employed the same basic layout as the Ago C I, but used the 220hp Benz Bz IV. Only built in relatively modest numbers, the Ago C II began to be deployed at the end of 1915 and operated on the Western Front. This C II, 371/15, is a late production example. The type's top level speed was quoted as 86 mph at sea level. (Cowin Collection)

A fine shot of the rarely pictured two seat, pusher-engined **Friedrichshafen FF37**, or **C I** to give it its military designation. Of early 1916 vintage, the experimental FF37's general layout appears to have been influenced by that of the Royal Aircraft Factory's F.E.2, following the British practice of seating the gunner in the nose, forward of the pilot. The FF37 was destined never to progress beyond the prototype stage. (Cowin Collection)

This close-up of the crew accommodation of a **Hansa-Brandenburg C I** can be dated to late 1916 or after, thanks to the presence of the pilot operated 8mm Schwartlose machine gun over the upper wing. The ring mounting of the observer's flexibly-mounted Schwartlose is just visible to the left of his forearm. This type was built exclusively in Austria by Hansa-Brandenburg's local subsidiary and the aircraft's Austro-Hungarian Air Service serial, 64.07, further identifies it as being the seventh of a sub-contracted production batch built by UFAG. Most C Is employed a 160hp Austro-Daimler. Operationally deployed initially in early 1916, the C I's modest

87mph top level speed at sea level may not have impressed, but its high altitude capability did. With an operational ceiling of 19,030 feet, the C I, once at height was largely impervious to interception. This helps explain why the type was never quite usurped by the later and faster Aviatik C I and remained operational until war's end. (Cowin Collection)

Below Whereas the **Ago** C I to C III had all been twin-boom fuselage designs, their **C IV** was of fairly conventional layout, the only novelty the pronounced degree of taper on the one-and-a-half bay wings. Generally well regarded by its crews, the C IV used a 220hp Benz Bz IV, giving it a top level speed of 119mph at 4,000 feet; normal range was 497 miles. Production bottlenecks, attributed to wing assembly, limited deliveries to around 70 operational examples. This is an early example, with balanced rudder and no fixed fin. (Cowin Collection)

Below A **Lloyd C II** of the Austro-Hungarian forces operating at the southern end of the Eastern Front in 1916. Seen here being re-assembled after being rail freighted to the front, little more information concerning the aircraft's, crew's or unit identity survives. However, photographs reveal that shortly after this image was taken, the machine nosed-over during the subsequent attempted take-off. (Cowin Collection)

Below This example of a late production **Ago C IV** was clearly cosidered something of a trophy by its No 32 Squadron, RFC, captors. This machine, C8964/16, captured on 29 July 1917, was flown to Britain for detailed evaluation, but crashed on 17 August 1917. Note Ago's adoption of a Sopwith style fixed fin on the later C IVs. (British Official/Crown Copyright)

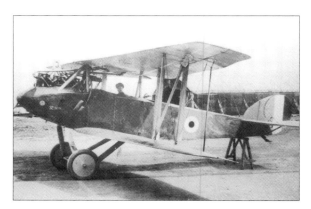

Above **Rumpler C I**, 53/16, powered by a 160hp Mercedes D III. Armed with a fixed, pilot-aimed 7.9mm Spandau, along with the observer's 7.92mm Parabellum, the Rumpler C I was considered by many to be the best and most reliable of all C types produced. Top level speed of the machine was 94mph at sea level, while the service ceiling was around 16,600 feet. Normal range was given as 336 miles. (Cowin Collection)

Opposite, top The tethered, or kite balloon had been seen as a valuable tactical reconnaissance tool long before the aeroplane's arrival and the German army continued to employ them right up until the Armistice. Although at first sight so vulnerable, the

employment of in-depth flak and other defences around each balloon made them particularly thorny prey for enemy attackers. Capable of day or night operation, the **German Type AE** balloon, seen here, was introduced during the early summer of 1916. Copied from the French Type M, the AE could be flown in winds of up to 55mph. With its greater lift, the AE could loft a considerable amount of gear, as well as its observer, within its basket, including radio telephony equipment and a long distance camera. Thus, on the AE, the parachute fitted was of suffient size to ensure the safe return not just of the observer, but of the whole basket's contents. At the end of 1916, no less than 128 single balloon sections, or Feldluftschiffer Abteilungen, were operationally deployed, usually being fielded in a well spread group of three to aid triangulation. (Cowin Collection)

This **Albatros C III** has clearly landed on the wrong side of the lines and provides the focus of interest for a number of French civilians, while the soldier in the foreground and close to the photographer appears more concerned with grooming his moustache. (Cowin Collection)

Below Deployed operationally for the first time towards the end of 1916, the **Albatros C III** was built in larger quantities than any other of the firm's C types. The C III, with its 160hp Mercedes D III had an undistinguished top level speed of 82mph at sea level. The initial single, flexibly-mounted 7.92mm gun was later supplemented by another, fixed forward-firing weapon for the pilot. In spite of its robust construction that allowed it to withstand considerable combat damage, the C III compared poorly in terms of performance with the DFW C V that was to become the main workhorse of the two seater units from late 1917 until the end of the war. (Cowin Collection)

Overleaf, top An excellent rear-on image of an **Albatros C III**, showing the standard multi-colour hexagonal lozenge camouflage adopted from January 1918 for use by all reconnaissance and fighter types in service with the German Imperial Army Air Service. (Cowin Collection)

Below A dramatic ground-to-air image of the 1916 **LVG C IV**. This type proved to be another reconnaissance design that failed to progress beyond the developmental stage. Powered by a 220hp Mercedes D IV, the LVG C IV appears to have been little more than a slightly scaled-up, more powerful variant of the widely used LVG C II. (Cowin Collection)

Opposite, below The **LFG Roland C II** of exceptionally clean appearance made its debut in October 1915 and stayed in front-line service until the autumn of 1917. Powered by a 160hp Mercedes D II, the C II's top level speed was 103mph at sea level. Thanks to its relatively short span, low aspect ratio wings, its high altitude performance was limited to a modest ceiling of 13,100 feet. This said, it should be noted that the RFC ace, Albert Ball cites this machine as being the best of the German two seaters with very effective fields of fire to the front and to the rear. This is an early production example, serving with Fl Abt A 227 at Lille in the autumn of 1916. The crew members are Lt Stuhldreer, pilot, sitting on the inboard upper wing, along with Lt Allmenroder, observer, astride the port wheel. (Cowin Collection)

Top, right Built in substantial numbers, the **Albatros C VII** entered operations near the close of 1916. Hastily developed to circumvent the engine-related unreliability being experienced by their C V, the C VII used the 200hp Benz Bz IV. With this engine, the C VII proved reliable and equally at home doing relatively high level reconnaissance at its ceiling of 16,400 feet, or doing its infantry support task of strafing trenches with its short range 200lb bomb load. At least 350 Albatros C VIIs had been delivered by the parent company and its two sub-contractors by February 1917. (Cowin Collection)

Rear aspect of a late production **LFG Roland C II** that complements the front view opposite. The salient difference between early and late machines is the increase of both fin and rudder area. The machine seen here belonged to the the Bavarian Fl Abt 292 and was photographed in early 1917. (Cowin Collection)

Overleaf The **Rumpler C III** two seater was a development of the widely used C I with the one major difference that it lacked any form of fixed fin. In the event, this deletion was to be the design's downfall. Using a 220hp Benz Bz IV, the C III entered service in early 1917, but was withdrawn from operations within a month or so following a spate of crashes, attributed to the machine's lack of adequate latitudinal, or

yawing control at low speed. It is reported that around 75 C IIIs had been delivered by Rumpler prior to the type's withdrawal from service. (Cowin Collection)

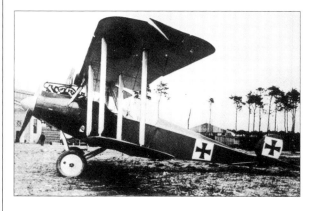

If the Rumpler C III had proven to be a disaster waiting to happen, its successor from the same stables was just the reverse. Powered by a 260hp Mercedes D IVa, the **Rumpler C IV** followed closely upon the C III, ensuring that the firm was in a position to continue producing two seaters almost without interruption during the spring of 1917. The C IV, with its top level speed of 109mph at sea level, combined with a superb high altitude capability of 21,000 feet saw the C IV providing stalwart service through to the cessation of hostilities. (Cowin Collection)

Opposite page Germany's leading World War I fighter ace, **Baron Manfred von Richthofen**, went to war in August 1914 as a young lieutenant in a lancer regiment, aged twenty two. Only at the close of 1914 did he succeed in transferring to the Army Air Service, where, as with many other fighter aces to be, he cut his aviation teeth first training and then operating as an observer. Indeed, it is generally held that although officially unconfirmed, his first 'kill' was made against a Farman from the rear of a two seater. Even after gaining his wings on Christmas Day 1915, the young flier was to remain piloting two seaters for much of 1916. It was during this period that he was to meet the father of German fighter tactics, Oswald Boelcke. Clearly something about Richthofen impressed Boelcke, who subsequently invited him to join his newly formed fighter squadron, or Jagdstaffel 2. Here, Richthofen was one of four to fly the

unit's first mission on 17 September 1916, setting him on a course that was to see him credited with 80 victories, before he and his scarlet Fokker Dr I were to meet their end on 21 April 1918. The Baron scored official victory number 16 on January 4 1917 and received the Pour Le Merite twelve days later as the new leader of Jasta 2 (at that time the medal was awarded for 16 kills). The picture captures the young Baron about to climb into his personal transport, which, ironically, was the sole prototype Albatros C IX, presented to him after its failure to gain full operational acceptance. (Cowin Collection)

The sole **Albatros C IX** of early 1917 was one of a number of prototypes submitted against the need for an armoured close air support type, shortly to be given their own CI designation to identify their specialised ground attack capability. As it transpired, the Junkers J I was to sweep all competition aside and, thus, the lone Albatros passed into the hands of Baron Manfred von Richthofen, for use as his personal transport. The 160 hp Mercedes D III powered C IX had a top level speed of 96.3mph. (Cowin Collection)

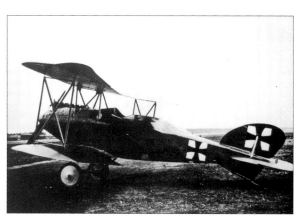

Another of the losing designs for the the armour clad, ground attack requirement was this one-off **Zeppelin-Lindau CI I**. First flown on 3 March 1917, this 160hp Mercedes D III two seater was the brainchild of a design team headed by Claudius Dornier and used the light alloy construction he was pioneering with his series of giant flying boats, dealt with in the next chapter. The Dornier CI I's top level speed was 102mph at sea level. (Cowin Collection)

Above The clear winner of the early 1917 close air support type competition was the extremely well armoured **Junkers J.4**, confusingly given the military designation, not of Cl I, but **J I**. For a 200hp Benz Bz IV powered aircraft, the J I was both big and heavy, built to withstand the withering close-range defensive fire likely to be encountered, ranging from rifle to heavy machine gun. First flown on 27 January 1917, the J I employed the Junkers pioneered thick aerofoil wing that provided more lift than a thin sectioned wing of comparable area. With a top level speed of 96mph at sea level, the J I was neither fast nor agile. However, it was very effec-

tive in its role and much beloved of its crews, whose sense of well-being owed much to the demonstrable protection provided by the machine's armour cladding. From the offensive viewpoint, the J I was fairly well equipped for its mission, carrying two, pilot-aimed, fixed forward firing 7.92mm Spandau, plus the observer's 7.92mm Parabellum, along with underwing racks for light bombs. The J I's biggest problem lay not so much with the machine, but its makers, who were better researchers than production engineers: thus, initial deployment did not occur until September 1917 and despite the clamour for more, only 227 had been built by the time of the Armistice in November 1918. (*Cowin Collection*)

Opposite, below Probably one of the best of the C types, **DFW's C V** embodied all of the neatness and efficiency of the C IV that had made its service debut early in 1916, but benefitted from the greater power of a 200hp Benz Bz IV. This gave the machine a top level speed of 97mph at 3,280 feet, while the C V's operational ceiling was 16,400 feet. Built not just by DFW, but by four other sub-contractors, the C V was probably the best all-rounder of the German two seaters with just under 1,000 being in operation on every front at the end of September 1917. Armament comprised the standard fixed, forward-firing and flexibly-mounted 7.92mm guns, plus light bombs. Shown here is a DFW C V of Fl Abt (A) 224 at Chateau Bellingcamps photogaphed on 22 May 1917. (Cowin Collection)

Lieutenants Leppin and Basedow, of Fl Abt 234, pose beside Aviatik-built DFW C V just prior to the launch of the great German offensive of late march 1918. Aimed at thrusting through to the French coast to sever contact between the British and French armies, the role of the Field Flight Sections in providing tactical information was crucial in the run-up to the 21 March zero hour. To this end, 49 Field Flight Sections, or approximately one third of Germany's total two seater assets were directly deployed in support of the offensive. The DFW C V was the mainstay of the field Flight Sections until into the summer of 1918 and the operational arrival of the DFW C VI. (Cowin Collection)

This **LVG C V** two seater has been flown to England for test and evaluation after its capture. First flown in early 1917, the LVG C V was deployed operationally during the summer of 1917. A sturdy design, the machine was well liked by its crews despite the somewhat restricted visibility it offered to both pilot and observer. Powered by a 200hp Benz Bz IV, the C V had a top level speed of 105mph at sea level, along with an impressive ceiling of 21,060 feet. Pilot and observer both had a 7.92mm machine gun. While no precise figures survive, several hundred LVG C Vs are known to have been built. (British Official/Crown Copyright)

One of the early production **Austrian Aviatik C I** two seat reconnaissance machines, used on the Italian Front in late 1917. The serial, 37.40, just visible on the fuselage, follows the Austro-Hungarian practice of using the first 2-digit group to denote the production batch, while the last two numbers signify the individual aircraft's place within the batch, in this case the 40th machine. Unlike the German system, there is no indication of the year in which construction took place. Sadly, little hard performance data survives on the type itself. (Cowin Collection)

Overleaf The **Albatros C XII** long range reconnaissance machine made its debut in the summer of 1917 and initial service deliveries commenced towards the end of that year. Power was provided by a 260hp Mercedes D IVa, giving the aircraft a top level speed of 109mph at sea level. The service ceiling for the C XII was cited as 16,400 feet. The standard

armament of single fixed and flexible 7.92mm guns was carried. This is the prototype, C1096/17. Albatros, plus three sub-contracting companies were involved in producing these machines, but quite how many is unknown. (Cowin Collection)

Below The **Hannover Cl IIIa** of 1918 was a relatively minor development of the company's Cl II and both used the same 180hp Argus As III. Both the Cl II and III series of ground attack and escort fighters endeared themselves to their crews thanks to a number of useful attributes. From the pilot's viewpoint, visibility was excellent both forward and downward, while the quaint biplane tail, with its narrow span and position, provided the observer with an improved rearward arc of fire. Top level speed of the Cl IIIa was 103mph at sea level, while the machine had a range of 285 miles. Agile and robust, the first of 439 Cl IIs entered service in December 1917, followed by 80 Cl IIIs and

537 Cl IIIas. Incidentally, the reason for the small number of Cl IIIs produced had nothing to do with the aircraft, but rather it was because it used a 160hp Mercedes D III, which was urgently needed to power the Fokker D VII. The standard two-gun armament, one for each crew member, was fitted. (Cowin Collection)

Right **August Rottau**, seen here on the right, who held the rank of sergeant pilot, came from flying on the Eastern Front to join Battle Section, or Schlachtstaffel 37 in February 1918. Holder of the Golden Military Cross of Merit, Rottau was credited with two confirmed 'kills'. Alongside Rottau in this photograph is his observer, Lt Perleberg. In German bomber and reconnaissance units, the observer's status was higher, with the pilot considered akin to a mere chauffeur. The task of the Battle Sections, of which there were 38 in March 1918, was to provide close, low-level air support at, and immediately behind, the enemy's front. (Cowin Collection)

Wings over the Water

When the German Imperial Naval Air Service went to war on 3 August 1914, it had long been decided that its primary asset would be the airship, with the aeroplane taking a very secondary place in the overall scheme. The role of the naval airship had also been defined prior to the war, in that it should undertake both strategic and tactical reconnaissance for the fleet, while also being employed for bombing missions. At the time, the navy had lost two of its three airships during the previous year, Zeppelin L 1 to lightning with the loss of 14 of the 26 aboard, no fatalities being associated with the destruction of Zeppelin L 2. While naval airship crews had flown training missions in commercial Zeppelins for a number of years, operational

experience for the warlike purposes now expected of them was extremely scant, thanks to the two 1913 losses, coupled to the fact that Zeppelin L 3 had only joined the navy in May 1914, less than three months prior to the declaration of war on France.

If this was the somewhat parlous state of naval airship activity, the naval aeroplane community was doing little better, with the 1914 edition of Janes' All The World's Aircraft listing the total German naval aeroplane inventory in early 1914 as consisting of 46, of which 36 were seaplanes. Similarly, to provide further perspective on the scale of German naval aeroplane activity, it should be noted that the same journal lists the total number of naval aviators as just 22 up to 31 March 1914. Further, unlike

the army, who had set aviator training as one of the priorities during 1912, the navy had just the one Johannisthal flying school and only expanded training through the use of civilian establishments after 3 August 1914.

Once at war, the Imperial Naval Air Service set about fulfilling the tasks it had been set with an ever growing degree of professionalism. By the time of the Armistice in early November 1918, the Service had grown beyond all recognition. To cite just a few figures showing the degree of expansion, at the close of the war, the aeroplane inventory had grown to around 1,500 of which approximately a half were front-line types, these being operated by 2,116 fliers. As for the naval airship community, this had grown to 16 airships and around 6,000 men. Here, however, it is sobering to reflect that these 16 lighter-than-air craft represented exactly a quarter of the 64 airships delivered to the navy during the war, giving some idea of the attrition in both men and airships suffered by this branch of the service.

Main picture Perhaps, psychologically it was the sheer affinity in terms of scale of the airship to that of their capital ships that led the German Imperial Naval Air Service to emerge from World War I still championing these goliaths of the skies, long after the German Army had foresaken them as being too costly in terms of manpower and resources, as well as being generally vulnerable. Certainly, the navy and the army's initial operational deployment of airships had provided very different experiences, with the army losing a half of its warworthy dirigibles within the first month of the conflict. The navy had no such early losses, in part, because they were only to accept their first two operational airships, L 4 and L 5, on 28 August and 22 September 1914. Certainly, by the end of 1916, naval airship losses were matching those of the army. Typical of the fate likely to befall an airship was that of the navy's **Zeppelin LZ 72**, naval designation **L 31**. The second of the Zeppelin 'r' class, built exclusively for naval operations and deliveries of which had started in May 1916, the L 31 had a crew of 17 and was powered by six 240hp Maybach H-S-Lu petrol engines giving a top level speed of 50mph. The range of the 'r' class was 5,000 miles. First flown on 12 July 1916, L 31 was dispatched to bomb London on 1 October 1916, only to fall in flames near Potters Bar just north of its target, prey to the guns of Lieutenant W.J. Tempest, RFC in his BE 2c. None of L 31's airshipmen survived. Equally telling is the fact that L 31 was one of 11 naval airships sent to bomb English targets that blustery night and of these, only seven managed to cross the enemy coast, six overflying Yorkshire. (Cowin Collection)

Below Five of these two seat **Gotha WD-1** reconnaissance floatplanes, No.s 285 to 289, were built for the navy in mid-1914. Fitted with a 100hp Daimler D I, the WD-1 had a top level speed of 56mph at sea level. If this seems low, the climb to 3,200 feet took a tedious 24.5 minutes. However, the WD-1 did appear to have, for its day, a useful range of 335 miles. Seen here is the prototype WD, the 100 hp Gnome powered prototype, first flown in February 1914 and which never seems to have been given a naval serial number. (Cowin Collection)

Overleaf This May 1915 photograph shows an Imperial Naval Air Service NCO observer, armed with rifle, about to take his front seat position in an **Albatros B I**. This extremely atmospheric image illustrates two important points. First, the aircraft, serial S77, belongs to the the Naval Landplane Section based at

Morseele, showing that the navy were early to establish a presence, alongside their army comrades, at the front, which they maintained until the end of the war. The second point is that prior to the arrival of the armed C types, with their flexibly mounted machine gun for the observer, both observers and pilots of the unarmed B type two seaters armed themselves with a motley range of personal weapons. (Cowin Collection)

Perpetrator of well over half a million pounds worth of damage to London in a single raid, the **L 13** was considered by the Naval Air Service to be its most successful airship. First flown on 23 July 1915, the L 13 was the seventh of the 22 Zeppelin 'p' class dirigibles, deliveries of which started in April 1915. Powered by four 210hp Maybach C-X petrol engines, this class had a top level speed of 60mph, along with a range of 2,672 miles. Crew complement of the 'p' class was 18. Of the 22 airships the army and navy initially each took 11, although the army's LZ 88 was to be subsequently tranferred to the navy. The L 13 survived 159 flights, covering 42,842 miles, to be safely decommissioned on 25 April 1917. (Cowin Collection)

The serial 424 on the rear fuselage of this **Gotha WD-2a** identifies it as being one of the later production 'small wing' version, differentiated by the 'a' suffix. First flown in July 1914, the WD-2 and WD-2a, of which a total of 27 were built, used either a 100hp Benz Bz III, or a 150hp Rapp. Built for long range

reconnaissance, the WD-2a's top level speed was 59.5mph at sea level, while its range was 415 miles, an 80 mile improvement on that of the earlier WD-1. (Cowin Collection)

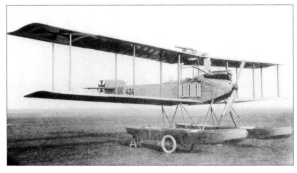

This **Gotha WD-2** was one of a small number of floatplanes the German navy handed over to its Turkish allies in 1916. Powered by a 150hp Benz Bz III, this machine carries an early, overwing gun mounting for its front seat observer, requiring him to stand when firing. (Cowin Collection)

The sole, experimental long range **Zeppelin-Lindau Rs I** flying boat was wrecked in a storm on 21 December 1915 before it could be flight tested. This three 240hp Maybach Mb IV-engined craft was the first of a series of one-off giant flying boats made feasible through the extensive use of light alloys, a field in which their creator, Prof Dr Claudius Dornier, one of Count Zeppelin's brighter proteges, had specialised. (Dornier)

The **Lohner Type L** two seater reconnaissance/bomber flying boat was used to real effect by the Austro-Hungarian Navy during the 1915-1916 period. Based on Jakob Lohner's 1913 Type E, the Type L was powered by various engines rated between

140hp and 180hp, giving the machine a top level speed of around 65mph. Thanks to its wing design, the Type L showed an impressive high altitude capability, having a ceiling of about 16,400 feet. Around 160 Type Ls were built, but such was their operational success that the machine was copied by Macchi in Italy, leading to the Macchi M.3 through M.9 series. (Cowin Collection)

Below The Naval Air Service's sole **Gotha WD-4**, 120. This three seat bomber owed much to the earlier Gotha G I built for the Army. First flown on 26 January 1916, the WD-4 typifies the seemingly haphazard procurement policy of the navy towards the purchase of aeroplanes for most of the war. Instead of buying a few types of aircraft and engines to meet their mission requirements, the navy bought a large variety of aeroplanes and engines in often very small quantities, making the maintenance crews' and supply people's lives a nightmare. Few performance details survive for the WD-4 other than that it had two 160hp Mercedes D III, giving it a top level speed of 85.5mph. Used spasmodically during 1916, the Zeebrugge-based WD-4, accompanied by five other seaplanes, was reported to have raided several ports in the south east of England, on 19 March 1916, ranging from Dover to Margate. (Cowin Collection)

The single **Zeppelin-Lindau Rs II** giant, long range flying boat is seen here in its initial form with biplane tail. First flown on 30 June 1916 with its three 240hp Maybach Mb IVs buried within its short, broad-beamed hull, the problem of power losses in the transmission must have been serious, leading to the Rs II's beaching for modifications. Centred around the engines, this work saw the replacement of the three buried units by four similar engines, now mounted between the hull and the parasol wing in twin push/pull nacelles, with each engine driving its propeller directly. The opportunity was also taken, at this time, to modify the machine's tail unit. In this later form and known as the Rs IIb, the flying boat got airborne once more on 6 November 1916. (Dornier)

Overleaf The **Zeppelin-Lindau Rs IIb**, seen here in almost final form and only awaiting its four 240hp Maybachs to be encased in drag-reducing engine nacelles. Capable of reaching 81mph top level speed at sea level, the Rs IIb had, by now, elicited sufficent naval interest to have been bought and issued with the serial 1433. Following flight testing, the machine was dismantled so that parts could be used in its successor, the Rs III. (Dornier)

Below Perhaps the best known **Friedrichshafen FF 33** of all was 'Wolfchen', or baby wolf, an **FF 33E**, serial 841, that served as the over-the-horizon eyes of the notorious German merchant raider, SMS Wolf. At sea for fifteen months, from 30 Novermber 1916, Wolf sank, or captured, 28 allied merchant ships, aided by the scouting efforts of 'Wolfchen's' crew, pilot Lt Strein and observer Oberflugmeister Fabeck, who made 50 sorties during the three ocean cruise. Incidentally, while at sea 'Wolfchen' flew with none of the national markings seen in this 6 March 1918 image, these only being restored after the Wolf's homecoming. With 162 examples of the FF 33E built, this was the most common version of all. Basic figures for the FF 33E indicate a top level speed of 78mph at sea level, along with a range of 340 miles. (Cowin Collection)

Right Even when the German navy found an aeroplane it liked, as in the case of the **Friedrichshafen FF 33** two seater, it seemed that it could not resist vacillating over equipment fit. Take the case of the FF 33 which was bought in larger quantities than any other naval aeroplane, here any economy-of-scale effect was largely dissipated, particularly early on, by buying small batches of differing versions. Thus, for those of a real 'rivet counting' persuasion, the contract history of the FF 33 makes superb reading, with the purchase of the first 247 aircraft involving 8 variants and no less than 42 contracts, none being larger than for 10 aeroplanes. For the record, total FF 33 deliveries amounted to 409 machines between December 1914 and October 1917. Shown here is a 33B being beached at Xanthi on the Black Sea in 1916.

The 33B was an unarmed reconnaissance version powered by a 160hp Maybach, giving it a top level speed of 68mph at sea level. Only five of this variant were ever ordered. (Cowin Collection)

Below True or false? If the original caption to this photograph is to be believed, the crew of this **Friedrichshafen FF 33H** are busy rescuing the crew of a downed enemy floatplane. There are, however, a number of anomalies if that is the case. First, there is a suspicious total lack of wing debris from the 'enemy' craft; and the distinct similarity of the two machines' floats indicates that the whole event was staged at some publicist's behest. An armed version of the FF 33E, some 40 FF 33Hs were built, the variant entering service in January 1916. Using the same 150hp Benz Bz III as that of the FF 33E, the FF 33H had a top level speed of 73 mph at sea level, along with a typical patrol endurance of around 5.5 hours. (Cowin Collection)

The **Hansa-Brandenburg FB** is yet another example of buying small numbers of many types. In this case, the navy purchased six only of this 150hp Benz Bz III powered two seat flying boat reconnaissance scout. Essentially a German-built version of the Lohner scouting flying boats, the performance details of the FB are lost, but its overall capability must have been close to that of the Lohner Type L. (Cowin Collection)

A starboard side view of **Sablatnig SF 2**, serial 580, photographed at Warnemunde on the Germany's Baltic coast. Employed as two seater advanced trainers, 580 was the first of 26 delivered to the German navy between June 1916 and May 1917. The SF 2's power was supplied by a 160hp Mercedes D III, giving the machine a top level speed of 81mph at sea level. (Cowin Collection)

Below Seven of these three seat **Gotha WD-7s**, 670 to 676, were built as torpedo-dropping trainers during 1916. Powered by two 120hp Mercedes DIIs, the machines had a top level speed of 85mph, while their normal operating range was 295 miles. The aircraft seen here was operated from the Norderney naval seaplane base. (Cowin Collection)

The sole **Albatros W 3**, serial 527, three seat torpedo bomber. Powered by two 160hp Mercedes D IIIs, the W 3 had a top level speed of 83mph at sea level. Delivered to the navy in July 1916, the W 3 led to the generally similar W 5 design, of which four were built and delivered between May 1917 and January 1918. (Cowin Collection)

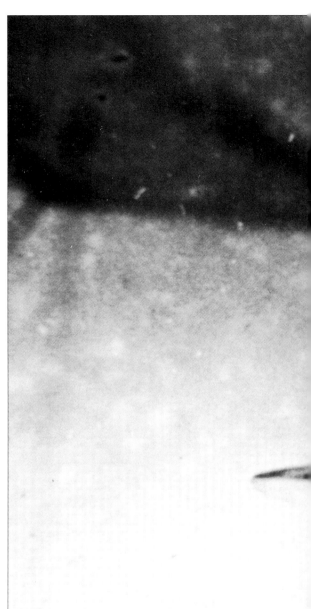

Right A single seat **Rumpler 6B2** floatplane fighter seen at its dynamic best. A lighter version of Rumpler's C I two seater and using the same 160hp Mercedes DIII, the original 6B1 entered service with the navy in July 1916, with deliveries continuing into 1917, when replaced in production by the 6B2 seen here. Just as the 6B1 had derived from the earlier C I, the 6B2 owed its genesis to that of the two seat Rumpler C IV. Overall, a total of 98 6Bs are reported to have been delivered when building ended in January 1918, comprising 43 6B1s and 55 of the 6B2 version. The top level speed of both versions was around 95mph and each carried a single, fixed, forward-firing 7.92mm Spandau. (Cowin Collection)

Above Used essentially for the local air defence of naval seaplane bases in the Flanders area, the single seat **Albatros W 4** float-plane fighter entered service with the navy in late 1916. Based on the company's successful D II fighter, but slightly scaled up, the W 4 used a 160hp Mercedes D III, giving it a top level speed of 109mph at 6,560 feet, dropping to 99mph at sea level. Armament comprised a single, synchronized 7.92mm Spandau, although some later machines carried a second gun. In all 117 W 4s were delivered, with 3 in 1916 and 114 in 1917. The machine seen here, serial 1512, was the penultimate of a 10 'plane batch delivered during October and November 1917. (Cowin Collection)

An in-flight image of the **Albatros W 4**, primary defender of the German naval seaplane bases around north west Europe from the end of 1916 through most of 1917, it being super-seded by the Hansa-Brandebburg W 12. (Cowin Collection)

Essentially a float-equipped version of the Ernst Heinkel-designed Hansa-Brandenburg KD/D I of early 1916, with added outboard wing bracing, the first of the navy's **58 Hansa-Brandenburg KDWs** was completed in September 1916. Typically, no less than three different engine types were fitted to the KDW, the initial 150hp Benz Bz III to the 13 aircraft, followed by the 160hp Mercedes D III in the next 10, while the last 35 machines received the 160hp Maybach Mb III. In the first 23 of these single seat fighters only one 7.92mm Spandau was fitted, whereas the last 35 mounted twin Spandaus. Top level speed was 106mph for the later fighters and range was cited as 310 miles. From a pilot's viewpoint, the KDW was not highly thought of, having virtually none existent visibility directly forward. (Cowin Collection)

Friedrichshafen FF 41A, serial 676, the first of three of these three-seat torpedo bombers to be built for the navy in late 1916-early 1917. Seen here at Zeebrugge on the Belgian coast, the FF 41A used two 150hp Benz Bz IIIs, giving it a top speed of 77.7mph, with a range of 357 miles. (Cowin Collection)

Little more than a cleaned up, 160hp Benz Bz IIIa-engined Gotha WD 9, their two seat **WD 13** coastal patroller was bought by the navy in 1917 specifically for Turkish use. Built only in small numbers, the WD 13's top level speed was 87mph, the machine had a useful operational range of 466 miles. (Cowin Collection)

Bottom An excellent air-to-air aspect on a two seat **DFW C V** of the German Imperial Air Service's 1st Field Service Section. Taken near to the front lines in the autunm of 1917, this view shows the irregular application of dull green and brown with which the majority of German combat types were camouflaged prior to the January 1918 adoption of the multi-colour hexagonal scheme. Both the 1st and 2nd naval Field Service Sections appear to have used a mixture of DFW C Vs and LVG C Vs with which to carry out their reconnaissance work. (Cowin Collection)

The single seat **Hansa-Brandenburg W 16** floatplane fighter was Ernst Heinkel's second fighter design of 1916, the earlier one being the company's KDW/W 11. Neat and compact, the W 16 incorporated a number of superior design features to its immediate predecessor, but despite this, orders for only three examples, serials 1077 to 1079, were to be received from the navy. Powered by a 160hp Oberursal rotary, the W 16's top level speed was 106mph at sea level. Seen here is the first of the three W 16s, 1077. (Cowin Collection)

The **Hansa-Brandenburg W 12**, another of Ernst Heinkel's creations, was a float-equipped, two seat reconnaissance fighter that first flew in January 1917 and started to replace the single seat Albatros W 4 from April 1917 onwards. Powered by either a 150hp Benz Bz III or 160hp Mercedes D III, the W 12 had a top level speed of 99.4mph and a ceiling of 16,400 feet. The machine seen here, serial 2016, was a Benz-equipped early production example. Armament comprised one, later two fixed, forward-firing 7.92mm Spandaus, plus the observer's flexibly mounted 7.92mm Parabellum. W 12 deliveries began in April 1917 and ended in March 1918, totalling 145 machines, excluding the prototype that had been destroyed early in flight testing. (Cowin Collection)

Below Something of an all-rounder, the **Gotha WD 14** is seen here in prototype form, wearing its naval serial 801. First flown in January 1917, this twin 220hp Benz Bz IV three seater was designed to fulfil the roles of torpedo bomber, minelayer, or long range reconnaissance. Top level speed was 72mph at sea level, while the range was an impressive 806 miles. Following satisfactory testing and acceptance of the prototype, a further 68 production WD 14s were delivered with the navy serials 1415-1430, 1617-1631, 1651-62 and 1946-1970. (Cowin Collection)

Typifying the perils of being an airshipman, is the all too brief career of navy **Zeppelin L 48**. The first of five Zeppelin 'u' class dirigibles, L 48 made its first flight on 22 May 1917. Based at Nordholz for its less than one month operational life, L 48 was to fall to the guns of Lt L.P. Watkins near the village of Theberton in Suffolk on 17 June 1917. Of the 19 crew, 3 were to survive. Powered by five 240hp Maybach H-S-u engines, the 'u' class airships had a top level speed of 71mph. (Cowin Collection)

The twin 150hp Benz Bz III powered **Albatros W 5** floatplane torpedo bomber came into naval service in May 1917 Capable of 83mph top level speed at sea level, four of these three man biplanes were built, serials 846 to 849, delivery ending in January 1918. The view of the second aircraft, 847, shows the machine's pusher engine configuration and the torpedo stowed, semi-recessed, within the aircraft's belly. (Cowin Collection)

Two **Zeppelins** in their lair, with the one on the left being the navy's L 44, the other, an unidentified early army airship. L 44 was the first of the two 't' class Zeppelin built for the navy and which made its maiden flight on 22 February 1917. With their five 240hp Maybach H-S-Lu giving them a top level speed of 64.5mph, these 't' class dirigibles had a range of 7,150 miles. Their crew complement was 23 and none of these survived when, on 20 October 1917, L 44 fell in flames to French artillery fire over Luncville-St Clement. (Cowin Collection)

In all, 80 of these **Hansa-Brandenburg W 29s** were to be delivered to the navy between December 1917 and July 1918, when production switched to the far higher powered W 33.

Initially powered by a 150hp Benz Bz III, later built W 29s had the up-rated 185hp Benz Bz IIIa, giving this two seat reconnaissance fighter a top level speed of 109mph. Climb to 3,280 feet took 5.9 minutes and the W 29's patrol duration was a respectable 4 hours. The twin white diagonal bands on the rear fuselage of this W 29 identify it as belonging to the Starboard Watch of the Norderney naval flying station. (Cowin Collection)

Zeppelin L 53 was the last of the Imperial Naval Air Service's airships to fall to enemy action in World War I. Entering service on 21 August 1917, this craft, the first of ten 'v' class Zeppelins, carried a crew of 19 and, under the impetus of its five 240hp Maybach H-S-Lu engines achieved a top level speed of 67mph. The operating range of these 'v' class ships of the sky was 8,390 miles. L 53 was to sortie some 50 times prior to falling victim to the guns of Lt S.D. Culley's Sopwith Camel on 11 August 1918. Headed out over the North Sea, L 53's crew had the misfortune to encounter a totally new form of menace, in the shape of the destroyer-towed, lighter-launched interceptor, a novel range-extending technique first demonstrated by Culley a few days earlier, on 31 July 1918. Using this method, Culley intercepted the Nordholz-based L 53 seawards of Terschelling, sending the dirigible flaming into the sea. There were no survivors. (Cowin Collection)

Overleaf **Theodore Osterkamp** and Gotthard Sachsenberg were to share the honour of being the Imperial Naval Air Service's highest scoring fighter ace and Osterkamp is pictured here sitting on the portside wheel of his Fokker E V, 156/18. It was in this machine that Osterkamp was to score his 25th to 31st 'kills' during the last few months before the Armistice. This, however, was far from the end of Osterkamp's remarkable fighting achievements for he was to continue to fly and fight, alongside his friend Gotthard Sachsenberg in the Baltic campaign until October 1919. This 'unofficial' war in the east was a mobile, messy, disorganised affair and the number of Osterkamp's victories remains unknown. In 1940 and aged 48, Osterkamp, now commanding the Luftwaffe's 51st Fighter

Wing, once again flew into combat, adding a further six 'kills' and taking his total confirmed score to 37 victories. Unfortunately, for 'Uncle Theo' as his men called him, this was all too much for his superiors who insisted that his future activities be of the 'chairborne' variety. Interestingly, as in the case of a surprisingly large number of other future fighter aces, Theodore Osterkamp's career almost never got started. Born on 15 April 1892, he was rejected by the Prussian Army as unfit for military service at the outbreak of World War I, but, happily, found the Imperial Navy more medically tolerant and was accepted for their volunteer naval flying service. After training and flying as an observer for half of the war, Osterkamp gained his pilot's wings at the end of March 1917. In mid-April he joined the 2nd Naval Field Service Section at the front. Here, he promptly crashed his Albatros C I, but retrieved his reputation by defying orders and going back aloft in a single seat scout to score his first confirmed victory by downing an SE 5a. The start of 1918 saw Osterkamp commanding the 2nd Jasta of the newly formed Naval Field Wing. Incidentally, it speaks volumes of that earlier medical decision to classify Osterkamp as unfit to know that during September and October of 1918 he survived a bout of the particularly virulent form of influenza that was to become pandemic and kill millions. Theodore Osterkamp ended his military career as a Generalleutnant, the equivalant of a two-star General, or Air Vice Marshal, commanding the Luftwaffe's fighter forces in Italy. (Cowin Collection)

Below The parasol-wing **Fokker E V**, later **D VIII**, was to be the last of the famed line of Fokker fighters to see action in World War I. Winner of the second 1918 fighter competition, held in April, the E V was considered slightly tail-heavy, but otherwise pilots were well disposed towards its agility, excellent climb and well harmonized controls. Deliveries of this 110hp Oberursal rotary powered single seater, 115mph at sea level, commenced in mid-1918, the first six examples being rushed to the army's 1st Fighter Wing, JG I. Next to receive the E V was the crack Naval Field Wing, with examples going to wing leader Gotthard Sachsenberg along with his deputy, Theodore Osterkamp.

These early machines proved to have structural wing flaws and other problems that necessitated their temporary withdrawal from service. Returned to the front in October 1918, the opportunity for this new fighter to make its mark evaporated with the Armistice. Seen here is one of JG I's E Vs, serial 149/18, belonging to Lt Liebig, while that of Lt Osterkamp's was 156/18. (Cowin Collection)

The Dornier-designed **Zeppelin-Lindau RS IV** turned out to be the ultimate wartime refinement of this series of giant, long-range flying boats. Carrying a crew of six, including a mechanic in each of the twin engined nacelles to tend the parasol winged machine's four 270hp Maybach Mb IVa powerplants. Flight testing, commenced on 12 October 1918, had hardly got underway at the time of the Armistice, with the result that much of the RS IV's estimated performance had yet to be explored. At the time flight testing ceased, the machine had achieved a top level speed of 86mph. Significantly, many of the construction practices developed for these wartime designs, along with the characteristic push-pull tandem engine layout were to find their way into the post-war family of very successful Dornier long range flying boats, starting with the 8-tonne Wal and culminating in the elegant, four-engined Do 26. (Dornier)

The Fokker Scourge and Beyond

As the proverb says; necessity is the mother of invention - and perhaps appositely, as the German Chancellor put it in the Reichstag on 4 August 1914, attempting to justify the infringement of Belgian neutrality, 'Necessity knows no law' - so it was the French, with huge tracts of their northern and north eastern territory serving as advanced German airfields, who saw the need to stop German reconnaissance over-flights. Let there be no doubt, even before the war had largely ground to a halt after the first few weeks, the French were given plenty of first-hand evidence of how good German reconnaissance was. Furthermore, they, themselves, had similarly benefitted from the input of their own airborne reconnaissance in halting the first major German push aimed towards Paris. With their typical no-nonsense approach to problems, the French put a machine gun into a number of their two seaters and sent them off to shoot down the

German two seaters as expeditiously as possible. Indeed, a Taube proved to be the first victim of this advance, falling to the nose-mounted gun of an armed Voisin on 5 October 1914. The fighter had been born and all this long before the close of 1914.

There were, however, problems with many of these first generation fighters, especially those with a tractor, or nose-mounted engine, prime among which, it was soon discovered, being their inability to fire with any accuracy. Actually, this was a far more fundamental problem than many realised, centred on the fact that the pilot now had to do much more work to fly the aeroplane towards his target in such a manner as to provide his observer with a free field of fire and anticipate enemy evasion; this happening between machines of fairly evenly matched performance. Further, while the Cauldron, Farman and Voisin pusher-engined two seaters appeared to eliminate

the problem by giving the nose gunner an unlimited forward field of fire, the inherent drawbacks of added weight and drag that went with the pusher layout reduced speed and agility significantly. Thus, unless a pusher had an initial height advantage, enabling it to dive on its prey, it was unlikely ever to be able to close on the enemy. As the French saw it, what was needed was to remove the observer altogether and simply fix the gun where the pilot could reach it. Oh, and while doing this, why not fix the gun so that it could fire directly ahead through the propeller arc of a small, fast single seater, of which the French had many? The concept certainly had appeal, chief of which was the single seater's significant speed advantage and, therefore ability to close quickly. The problem now was to solve the business of firing a machine gun through the propeller without shooting its blades off. In this regard, a Swiss engineer had already patented a gun synchronization system in 1913 and Frenchman Paul Saulnier of Morane-Saulnier fame had started working on a similiar device prior to the outbreak of war, but while both systems looked fine on paper, neither of them wanted to work in practice. Clearly logic,

even of the French variety, had it limits. Pursuing 'Plan B', France turned to one of her most lauded aviators, Roland Garros. Maybe he could come up with a solution. After a few months he did. What he produced was far from ideal, but it worked. Garros and his mechanic, tired of trying to get the 'fidgety' Saulnier synchronizer to work, turned to Panard, the armoured vehicle builders, who knew a bit about armour cladding. Garros's solution was simple, why bother doing anything complicated, just clad the propeller blades with armoured cuffs and, hey presto, the bullets that did strike the cuff would be deflected while the rest sped off in the enemy's direction. To everyone's delight, when Garros and his mechanic tried this in early April 1915 it worked and this deflector system was widely employed on Morane-Saulnier Type Ns until the interrupter or synchronizer systems could be made to work. The really great bonus of simply having to point the aeroplane at the enemy and fire the gun was to reduce pilot workload back to almost the point it had been before the gun had made its advent. The first real fighter had been produced.

The deployment of these French single seat fighters gave them a significant tactical advantage over their German opponents, but only temporarily. On 18 April 1915 Roland Garros was compelled to land behind enemy lines and was captured before he could destroy his machine with its armour-cuffed propeller blade secret. While the Germans were not necessarily overly impressed by this less than elegant solution, they did see the merit of allowing the pilot to aim the whole aircraft at his prey. Anthony Fokker, who was already working on a gun interruptor system was induced to expedite completion. This he did in May 1915, fitting the equipment into one of his Fokker M5K reconnaissance two seaters. On 1 August 1915, Max Immelmann brought down a BE 2c over Douai using the Fokker interrupter gear in a Fokker Eindecker, taking the first step towards redressing the balance in the tactical airwar. A number of Fokker M5Ks were converted to gun-equipped E 1s and by the end of August 1915, the era of the so-called Fokker Scourge had begun. From September 1915, the somewhat underpowered E Is with their 80hp Oberursal rotaries, were augmented by the 100hp rotary powered E IIs and E IIIs, the last of the Eindeckers, the 160hp engined E IV emerging in January 1916. The belligerents on both sides now had effective single seat fighters, It was now up to men like Boelcke and Immelmann to define and refine the tactics of aerial combat. From this point on and for the rest of the war, fighter development continued apace, with one side or the other gaining temporary superiority with the introduction of their latest type, only to find it rendered obsolescent long before its successor could possibly be brought into service.

A near to pilot's-eye view of an experimental triple 7.92mm Spandau gun installation synchronized to fire through the propeller arc of this **Fokker E IV**. This fit was the culmination of Fokker's efforts to arm his early monoplanes, or eindeckers and although Max Immelmann tested this three-weapon fit, he preferred the Eindecker's standard single gun installation. (Cowin Collection)

Fokker E IIIs of KEK Vouziers, the KEK signifying KampfEinsitzer Kommando, comprising 16 aircraft, in this case, supporting the 3rd Army in the Vouzier sector. Initially the relatively few Fokker Eindeckers had been distributed in pairs to the Field Flight Sections, but were brought together to form the KEK from February 1916. However the KEK proved short-lived, being ended in October 1916, to make way for the squadron, or Jagstaffel system, which, while theoretically having 16 machines, frequently could only muster around 8. The Jagstaffel, usually abbreviated to Jasta, was to remain the basic fighter unit of the German army until the Armistice, although after mid-1917, these were operated more and more as part of a larger wing, or Jagdeschwader, normally shortened to JG, that comprised anything up to 60 aircraft. (Cowin Collection)

The **Fokker E III** of Max Immelmann at Douai, where his unit, KEK 3, was based. Immelmann had been the first to score a victory in a Fokker Eindecker in the autumn of 1915, when he and Oswald Boelcke were serving together as the single seater section of Fl Abt 62. Inventor of the Immelmann Turn, a basic air fighting maneuvre using a loop and roll to reverse the enemy's initial advantage if attacked from the rear, Oblt Max Immelmann, with 15 confirmed victories, was killed in air combat near Lens on 18 June 1916. Powered by a 100hp Oberursel U I rotary, the E III had a top level speed of 87mph at sea level. Armament normally comprised a single 7.92mm Parabellum or Spandau, although some E IIIs were known to carry a second. Around 260 E IIIs are believed to have been built. (Cowin Collection)

Kurt Student, like Boelcke and Immelmann, first came to the attention of his superiors thanks to his prowess flying a Fokker E III. Transferred with their E IIIs to the Russian Front in September 1915, Student and his companion soon found themselves unopposed whenever and wherever they flew. Later, Lt Student was to take command of Jasta 9 in 1917, staying as its

leader until the Armistice, by which time he held the rank of Oberleutnant, or 1st lieutenant and had a confirmed score of 5 'kills'. Student went on to command the German aiborne forces in World War II, a responsibility vested in the German air force, unlike its American and British opponents, whose armies retained full control of both glider and paratroop assets. Student is depicted here sitting in his Albatros D III soon after taking over Jasta 9. (Cowin Collection)

Anthony Fokker, seen here with his mother, in 1919, after his return to Holland. Fokker had built his first design, the Spin, towards the close of 1910, test hopping it and simultaneously making his first flight prior to Christmas. While away, a colleague wrecked this machine, but, undaunted, Fokker, with help, built a second Spin, this time with a rudder. It was in this aircraft that he gained his pilot's licence in May 1911. The jovial Fokker, born on 6 April 1890, soon proved to have more than his fair share of business acumen, one of his early shrewd moves being to leave his native Holland, at the close of 1911, to set up shop in Germany. Once there, his tireless self-promotion, supported by his not inconsiderably aerial bravado, helped keep his name and products prominent. Never one to miss an opportunity, his early military flying school venture brought not only much needed cash, but longer term influence in high places. Later, during the war, Fokker, some of whose designs were not held in the highest esteem, frequently held lavish entertainments for senior military staff on the top floor of

Berlin''s Hotel Bristol which he appears to have leased on a long term basis. In yet another example of his business initiative, Fokker, in the immediate wake of the Armistice, managed to commandeer a train and smuggle much of his plant's machine tools and a number of Fokker D VII airframes and engines across the neutral Dutch border. Fokker died on 23 December 1939. (Cowin Collection)

The joint brainchild of the Steffen Brothers, Franz and Bruno, the **Siemens-Schuckert Werke D 5** single seat fighter was completed in the autumn of 1915, but progressed no further than the prototype stage. Visible in the background is the same company's E I prototype, a developed version of which killed designer/pilot Franz Steffen in June 1916. (Cowin Collection)

The **Hansa-Brandenburg KD**, with its novel interplane strut layout earned the instant sobriquet of 'Star Strutter'. Completed at the start of 1916, the KD was Ernst Heinkel's first single seat fighter design. Small and rugged, the KD was soon selected by the Austrians to serve as their standard fighter. The D I, to give its Austrian designation, was built locally by Phonix and Ufag. Powered initially by a 160hp Austro-Daimler, later Ufag machines had a 185hp Austro-Daimler, giving the compact fighter an enviable top level speed of 116mph, along with an excellent initial rate of climb in excess of 1,100 feet per minute. One of the D I weaknesses centred on it single 8mm Schwarzlose machine gun's lack of reliability, the gun being mounted above the upper wing centre-section to fire clear of the propeller arc and, thus not reduce its rate of fire. Besides siring the D I, the KD went on to be bought by the German navy as the KDW floatplane fighter. In this guise, the machine

carried additional outboard 'V' wing struts. Deliveries of the approximately 200 D Is built began in the autumn of 1916 through early 1917, while deliveries of the 58 naval KDWs stretched from September 1916 to February 1918. The prototype, shown here in its initial form, has a fin that differs from those of production aircraft. (Cowin Collection)

The Fokker Scourge that had lasted nine months or so came to an end in the late spring of 1916, with the mass advent of the fast and agile Nieuport 17, for which the Eindeckers were no match. As was inevitable, an intact example of the Nieuport fell into German hands fairly soon after its debut. The German reaction was interesting. As quickly as possible the aircraft was stripped and engineering drawings produced. These, along with requests for tenders to produce a copy were issued to industry. Euler and Siemens-Schuckert Werke were the two companies selected to build this back-engineered version of the Nieuport. Depicted here is a line-up of five **Siemens-Schuckert Werke D Is**, fresh from final assembly, at the company's Nuremburg facility. Markedly inferior in performance to the original, the single seat D I used a 110hp Siemens Sh I rotary, giving a top level speed of 97mph at 6,560 feet. Originally, orders for 250 D Is had been placed with the firm, but these were progressively cut back to 94 by the spring of 1917. The D I was mainly delivered to the Eastern Front, being generally considered inferior to the newly developed Albatros D III. (Cowin Collection)

Very few records survive concerning the other Nieuport copy, the **Euler D.I**, other than the knowledge that it was powered by a 100hp rotary and, as this picture shows, that at least one

made it to the Western Front. This image was taken in July 1916 or immediately thereafter with KEK Nord, prior to it becoming Jasta 1 on 23 August 1916. The Euler's pilot, seen here, Lt Leffers, credited with one 'kill', was to meet his own end near Cherisy on 27 December 1916. (*Cowin Collection*)

Bottom A slightly more powerful version of **Halberstadt's** D I of late 1915, the **D II** entered service during the summer of 1916 as a replacement for the now obsolete Fokker Eindeckers. Powered by a 120hp Mercedes D II, its frail appearance belied what proved to be a robust structure. Top level speed of the D II was 90.1mph at sea level, while its operational ceiling was around 13,000 feet. Carrying a single 7.92mm Spandau, probably just over 100 D IIs were built by the parent company, plus Aviatik and Hannover. Halberstadt D II, 818/16, seen here, served on the Eastern Front. (*Cowin Collection*)

Below **Halberstadt D IIs** of Kampfgeschwader 1 operating from their base at Hudova in the Rumanian-Macedonia theatre of operations in 1916. (*Cowin Collection*)

Opposite Hauptmann **Oswald Boelcke**, pictured here sitting in his Fokker D III, 352/16, in which he led his newly formed Jasta 2, pending the arrival of the Albatros D I. Boelcke

commanded the unit between 1 September and his death, less than two months later, in an air-to-air collision on 28 October 1916. Born in Saxony on 9 May 1891, Oswald Boelcke, described as frail and bookish as a boy, joined a military academy in 1911, gaining a commission in August 1912. Already trained as a telegrapher, Boelcke transferred to the Imperial Army Air Service in mid-1914 to gain his wings days after the outbreak of war. Boelcke spent the rest of 1914 flying Albatros B IIs with Fl Abt 13. Early in 1915, Boelcke found himself temporarily grounded with asthma, leading to his spending two weeks in the Air Service Headquarters, where he was to make some extremely useful senior level contacts. Boelcke, on his return to flying, joined Fl Abt 62 with Albatros C Is and LVG B IIs. After an uneventful spring, the unit moved to the front in the early summer. On 4 July 1915 Boelcke's observer downed their first victim, a Morane-Saulnier Type L. Two days later Boelcke switched to flying the newly arrived Fokker Eindecker single seater, with it interrupter-geared fixed, forward-firing gun. Between then and 21 May 1916, Boelcke scored a further 17 confirmed victories, most of which were obsolescent two seaters. Incidentally, operating alongside Boelcke during this period was Fl Abt 62's other single seat section pilot, Max Immelmann. Between them the pair had well and truly opened the era of the Fokker Scourge. In November 1915, Boelcke was posted to the Air Service's Operational Headquarters, at Charlesville, for a three month attachment. Here, Boelcke's academic skills came into play as he wrote what was to become the standard German Fighter Pilot's Rule Book for the rest of the war. Promoted Hauptmann, or captain, in May 1916, Boelcke was rapidly becoming too valuable to be allowed to continue combat flying and he was sent east to lecture tour on air fighting tactics. On 1 July 1916, the British opened their Somme Offensive, leading to the front line air service units coming under mounting pressure. Boelcke, currently in Bulgaria, was recalled to flying duties as commander of Jasta 2, for whose formation and personnel selection he was responsible. Among those Boelcke selected to fly with him was a young man named Manfred von Richthofen, along with, ironically, Erwin Bohme, the man who was, inadvertently, the cause of Boelcke's death. Between 1 September 1916 and his death, Boelcke added a further 22 victories to bring his ultimate confirmed score to 40. (*Cowin Collection*)

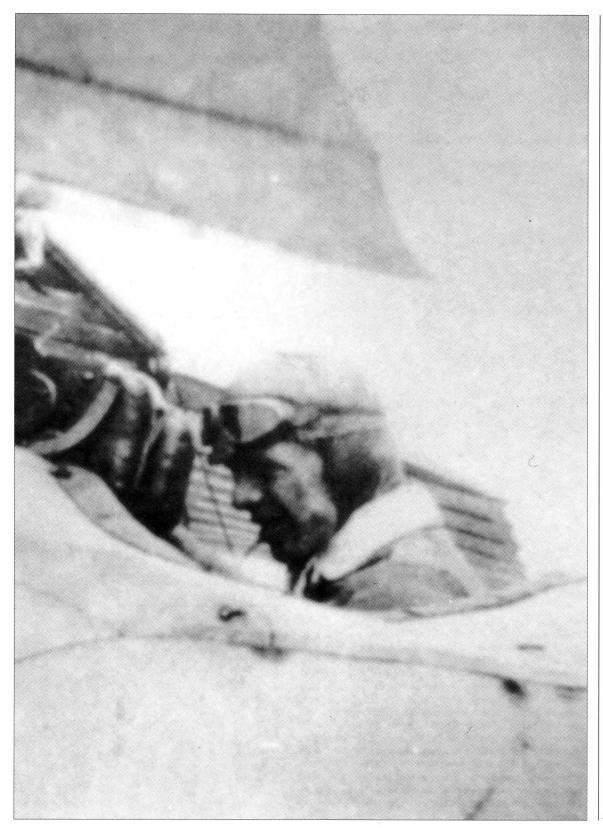

Right Although favoured by Germany first great air ace, Oswald Boelcke, who flew **Fokker D III** 352/16 and scored six of his forty victories in this machine, the type was not generally liked by front line pilots, perhaps because of a lack-lustre performance, not helped by Fokker's retention of wing warping, rather than ailerons. The Bavarian procurement authorities were even more critical, refusing to purchase the these Fokker biplanes at all until pressured from high places in Berlin. The Fokker D III made its operational debut in the spring of 1916 and, using the unreliable 160hp Oberursal U III, had a top level speed of 99mph at sea level. The D III was armed with two 7.92mm Spandaus. As an operational fighter, the career of the D III was brief, the type soon being relegated to advanced flying schools with many of the 230 built being delivered directly to training units. (Cowin Collection)

The period between the end of 1915 and the summer of 1917 can be seen as one of the low points in the fortunes of Fokker, the man and his company. This largely fallow time saw Fokker and his designers turn to biplane fighter designs, carrying the military designations D I to D V. As sometimes happens, the second of these, the rotary-powered **Fokker D II** was to emerge ahead of the in-line engined D I, of which only 25 were produced. Initially appearing at the front in the early spring of 1916, the D II was powered by a 100hp Oberursal U I. Armed with a single 7.92mm Spandau, the D II was woefully lacking in verve and agility, production being switched to the more powerful D III after only 61 examples of the D II had been built. (Cowin Collection)

The last of this series of comparative failures from **Fokker**, prior to the appearance of the much promoted Dr I triplane was the **D V**, the D IV never emerging as such. While the D V, of which 216 were built, showed far better pilot handling than its predecessors, it was deemed to be inferior to the Albatros D IIs just coming into service and, like its immediate forebears, was re-directed to advanced training units. Delivery starting at the close of 1916, the D V was powered by a 100hp Oberursal U I and carried a single 7.92mm Spandau. Top level speed of the D V was 107mph, but climb rate was a fairly tardy 19 minutes to reach 9,800 feet. (Cowin Collection)

Jasta 25's **LFG Roland D II** single seat fighters lined up on their Catnatlarzi base in Macedonia during 1917. First flown in October 1916, the twin 7.92mm Spandau armed D II was built in far greater quantities than either of the company's D I or D III designs. Like the D I, the D II used a 160hp Mercedes D III that gave a top level speed of 105mph at sea level. Entering service in early 1917, a total of around 300 D IIs are believed to have been built, both by LFG and Pfalz. The machine was not unconditionally loved by its pilots, who found it particularly sensitive, especially in the yawing plane. Incidentally, this image, showing as it does no less than ten D IIs, goes some way to refute the often made claim that no unit seems to have been exclusively D II-equipped. (Cowin Collection)

The **Albatros D II**, the fighter that turned the tide of the air war in Germany's favour, at least for a while. Albatros had first flown their prototype D I fighter during August 1916 in answer to a pressing need to counter the current ascendency of the Nieuports and DH 2s. Flight testing of the D I showed it to be

fast, agile and with an excellent climb rate. The type was rushed into production so fast, that the first service deliveries were being made to Jasta 2 by early September 1916! Powered by a 160hp Mercedes D III, the less than 100 D Is built proved capable of reversing the Allies former fighter superiority. Acknowledging constructive criticism from the front line pilots, Albatros set about improving forward visibility by slightly lowering the upper mainplane to produce the D II in December 1916. With the exception of the lowered upper wing, the two machines were virtually identical. Again, D IIs were rushed to the front as soon as they were completed and tested, with LVG Roland and Ufag helping to spread the production load. Well over 300 of these 109mph top level speed at sea level, twin 7.92mm Spandau-armed single seaters were to be built before production switched to the even better Albatros D III in early 1917.

A superb side view of a late production **Albatros D II**, 1076/17, still flying after 15 April 1918, as is immediately apparent from it having the angular Balkankreuse, or Greek Cross, in place of the earlier, curved Cross Patee. (Cowin Collection)

Opposite, top The **Albatros D III**, although having an entirely new wing, elsewhere embodied as much of the D II componentry as it could, revealing that Albatros's Chief Engineer, Robert Thelen's design philosophy lent towards doing things in an evolutionary, rather than a revolutionary manner. The D III can with hindsight be seen as the best of the Albatros single seaters, its successor, the D V incorporating too few real improvements over the D III at a time when the opposition was advancing apace. The D III, great aeroplane as it turned out, had one major inherent design flaw that led to wing flutter at high speed and consequent occasional structural failure and mid-air break up. The root of the problem lay in Thelen's decision to follow the Nieuport practice by adopting a sesquiplane, literally a one and a half wing layout. In doing this, Thelen fell into the same trap that the Nieuports had already experienced and had never really solved. In essence, the trouble lay with the combination of a torsionally weak, small lower wing being made to twist and oscillate through then little understood aerodynamic loads transmitted to it via the 'V' type interplane struts. This led to D III pilots being prohibited from diving the machine above a certain speed; quite a constraint for pilots who at some time or another were going to rely on the aircraft's ability to break away quickly from combat with a superior opponent. Shown here is an initial production model Albatros D III, delivered to Jasta 29 in early 1917. Although very kind in terms of pilot handling, these early D IIIs, besides being dive limited had another hazard in the form of the radiator that can just be seen positioned immediately ahead of the cockpit and filling the space between fuselage and upper wing centre section. If hit during combat, the radiator fluid could readily scald the pilot and frequently did. The solution was to move it to the underside of the upper starboard wing. In all, more than 1,300 D IIIs were built, the first being delivered to the front in January 1917. While the sea level top speed of the D III was the same as that

for the D I and D II, its speed at height was improved through the use of a high compression Daimler D III. Armament comprised the by-now standard twin 7.92mm Spandaus. The D III's heyday in the spring of 1917 began to fade by the summer when encountering the new Allied fighters in the shape of Sopwith Camels, Royal Aircraft Factory SE 5s and Spads. (Cowin Collection)

A later production **Albatros D III**, showing the new radiator position displaced to the starboard, underside of the upper wing centre section. (Cowin Collection)

Top right An extremely rare image, taken sometime after 15 April 1918, showing an **Albatros D III** fitted with additional small, load-spreading ancillary struts at the lower end of the normal 'V' interplane struts., clearly aimed at alleviating the high speed flutter problem. As these added struts have never appeared in any other picture of an Albatros D III seen by the author, he suspects that this fit was a locally devised modification. (Cowin Collection)

Lt **Hans Adam** of Bavarian Jasta 35, seen in the cockpit of his Albatros D III, 2101/16. Adam, with 21 confirmed 'kills', met his own end in the skies over Mortvilde on 15 November 1917, while flying with Bavarian Jasta 6. (Cowin Collection)

Overleaf This image of Offstv **Edmund Nathanael**, standing with his Albatros D III of Jasta 5, helps point up the fact that non-commissioned ranks formed a significant part of the total flying personnel strength, although perhaps less so in fighter units than elsewhere. Nathanael had scored 14 confirmed before being killed near Bourlon on 17 May 1917. (Cowin Collection)

This early production **Albatros D III** of Lt Dornheim, Jasta 29, having its radiator put under scrutiny. This image is also useful in showing the standard starboard side-only position of the Mercedes D III's exhaust manifold. (Cowin Collection)

The sole prototype **Zeppelin-Lindau V-1** single seat fighter, completed during the summer of 1916, was not just Claudius Dornier's first attempts at a fighter, but one of his first on any type of aeroplane. Of workmanlike, rather than elegant appearance, the finished product showed the influences of Nieuport's

sesquiplane wing layout, in a British-style pusher engined airframe. Using a 160hp Mercedes D III, the V-1, as to be expected of Dornier, employed an all-alloy structure. Sadly, someone had miscalculated the machine's dynamic, or in-flight balance. This was something the company's test pilot, Bruno Schroter, clearly suspected to be the case following his high speed taxying tests and he wanted nothing more to do with the V-1. The man found to make the the aircraft's maiden flight was Oblt **Hallen von Hallerstein**, a notable military flier, who had only recently completing the test flying of the giant Zeppelin-Staarken VGO III. Tragically, Schroter's prediction concerning the aircraft's tail-heaviness proved correct and on 13 November 1916, following lift-off, the V-1's nose continued to rise until the fighter stalled and fell to earth, von Hallerstein being killed in the crash. (Cowin Collection)

The story of the **Albatros D IV** is a tale of the one that got away. Following upon the operational success of their D II and D III fighters, Albatros came up with the extremely logical idea of using the robust wing of the D II, married to a new elliptical sectioned fuselage, later to be adopted for their D V. This hybrid machine was the Albatros D IV of which only one was built. Up to now, Albatros's thinking had been flawless, particularly as the reversion to the D II's wing promised to prevent the occasional catastrophic high speed wing shedding being experienced with their 'V' strutted D III sesquiplanes, as narrated above. Where Albatros's thinking went awry was in choosing to fit the prototype with an experimental geared variant of the 160hp Mercedes D III. This engine, which appears never to have worked satisfactorily, managed to delay D IV flight testing to the point where officialdom simply lost interest. With another engine, the D IV might have helped bridge the gap between the Albatros D III and the Fokker DVII, something the Albatros D V never quite did. (Cowin Collection)

Bruno Loerzer, an Oberleutnant at the time this picture was taken, when commanding Jasta 26 of JG 2. Born on 22 January 1891, Loerzer is seen standing besides his Albatros D V. Awarded the Order Pour Le Merite, Germany's highest military honour on 12 February 1918, Loerzer went on to become a Hauptmann, the equivalent to a US Captain or RAF Squadron Leader, when promoted to lead JG 3. Loerzer ended his war with an accredited 44 'kills', placing him 8th in the ranking of German leading air aces. (Cowin Collection)

Early in 1917, while the **Albatros** D IV saga was still unravelling, as dealt with above, the firm produced its first **D.V.** As it transpired, while adequate and built in massive numbers, this design served to prove the law of diminishing returns. In essence, the Albatros D V employed exactly the same wings as the D III, along with the tailplane and elevator, all of which were interchangeable between the two fighters. Initially, even the fin and rudder were identical, but later fin area was increased, leading the to the D V's characteristically rounded rudder trailing edge. Married to these components, Albatros took the new, semi-monocoque fuselage developed for their D IV and, for good measure, further lowered the upper wing in relation to the fuselage in order to yet further improve the pilot's forward visibility. The engine in early D Vs remained the 160hp Mercedes D III, replaced in the structurally strengthened D Va with the 185hp D IIIa. Both the German Air Ministry and Albatros appeared happy with the resulting machine, despite the fact that its top level speed of 116mph at 3,280 feet, or for that matter the fighter's agility, were little improved compared with the D III. Further, the high speed lower wing flutter of the D III was still present, restricting high speed flight and, therefore, limiting the combat pilot's primary option of diving away from trouble. The armament comprised the standard twin 7.92mm Spandaus. Initial deliveries of D Vs were made to the front in July 1917 and rapidly built up from that point on, with Albatros output being joined by that of their Austrian subsidiary OAW. During the autumn of 1917, D V production was switched to the strengthened and more powerful D Va. No precise production totals have survived for the D V and Va, but the knowledge that at their respective peaks of November 1917 and May 1918, no less than 526 D Vs along with 986 examples of the D Va were in service, would, allowing for attrition and spares, indicate a minimum overall build exceeding 2,200 machines. There is reason to believe that all 80 Jastas operating in the spring of 1918 had, at least, some D V or Va on their strength. The early D V depicted carries the Bavarian Lion motif of Hpt Eduard Ritter von Schleich, leader of Jasta 21, who survived the war with a Pour Le Merite ('Blue Max') and a confirmed 35 'kills'. The pilot's headrest, seen in this image, was not particularly favoured by operational pilots and was soon removed from most machines. (Cowin Collection)

Destined to head the Luftwaffe in World War II, **Hermann Goring** is pictured here, second from left, with his newly delivered Albatros D V. At this time Goring was serving with Jasta 27 and had just scored his fifth 'kill'. He was to finish the war as a Hauptmannn, commanding JG 1, the post he took over following the death of Baron Manfred von Richthofen. Goring was a holder of the Pour Le Merite and had 22 confirmed victories. (Cowin Collection)

An interesting frontal aspect on the **Albatros D Va**, believed to have belonged to a Bavarian Jasta and which from the presence of wheel chocks and the mechanic holding the tail down is seen undergoing engine running tests. (Cowin Collection)

Above **Lt Schlomer** poses nonchalantly beside his **Albatros D Va** in the late summer of 1917. Schlomer had became leader of Jasta 5, following the death of Oblt Berr at Noyelles on 8 April 1917. Schlomer, himself was to be killed just over a year and a month later, on 31 May 1918. (Cowin Collection)

The other side of the coin. To counterbalance the romantic view of air combat is this image of the debris of what had been Oblt **Hans Berr's Albatros D V**, in which he was killed south of Noyelles on 6 April 1917. Berr had been the first commanding Officer of Jasta 5 and died with a confirmed score of 10 victories. (Cowin Collection)

Below Oberleutnant **Freidrich Ritter von Roth**, seen here standing beside his Albatros D Va, was born of aristocratic parents on 29 September 1893. Having volunteered at the outbreak of war, 'Fritz', as he was popularly known, joined a Bavarian artillery regiment and was almost immediately promoted to sergeant. Wounded in action soon after, Roth was

commissioned on 29 May 1915 while still recuperating. Transferring to the flying service and pilot training towards the close of 1915, Roth was severely injured in a flying accident that delayed his gaining his wings until early 1917. Roth's first operational experience was gained with Fl Abt 296, a two seater unit, then based at Annelles, as part of the 1st Army, which he joined on 1 April 1917. Roth moved to fighters in the autumn of 1917 and after a busy closing quarter of 1917 and early 1918, during which he had served with Jastas 34 and 23, he was given command of Jasta 16 on 24 April 1918. Meanwhile, Roth's first confirmed 'kill' was made on 25 January 1918 and involved the dangerous business of downing a heavily defended balloon. As balloons were considered a vital tactical reconnaissance tool by both sides and were always heavily defended, it is a measure of the man that Roth appears to have subsequently specialized in attacking balloons, being credited with no less than 20 of them out of his total 28 confirmed vicories. Dispirited by the impact of the Armistice and the dissolution of his beloved Air Service, Freidrich Ritter von Roth took his own life on New Year' Eve, 31 December 1918. (Cowin Collection)

Top right With only a handful built, the **AEG D I** was one of the rarer types to find its way into front-line service with the single seater units during the latter half of 1917. Armed with twin 7.92 Spandaus and powered by a 160hp Mercedes, this diminutive fighter had a useful top level speed of 124mph, but this could well have been counter-balanced by poor climb, tricky handling and longish take-off requirement, if the machine's wing loading was as high as the photograph would suggest. The AEG D I, 4400/17, shown here belonged to Lt **Walter Hohndorf**, leader of Jasta 14. It was in this fighter that Hohndorf crashed to his death on 5 September 1917, after a combat in which he had scored his 12th 'kill'. (Cowin Collection)

Below First flown around June 1917, the clean-looking **Pfalz D III** , like its near contemporary, the Albatros D V, was to prove inferior to the Camel, SE 5 and Spad that were to be encountered in ever growing numbers from the summer of 1917 onwards..Initially deployed operationally in late August 1917, the 160hp Mercedes D III-powered machine lacked the agility and climb capability of the Albatros D V, but was faster than the D V, having a top level speed of 112mph at sea level, falling to 103mph at 9.840 feet. Further, the Pfalz D III was extremely robust and suffered none of the wing flutter problems of the Albatros series. It was therefore useful for fast attack missions such as those against well defended balloons. The one area that pilots were particularly critical of in the D III was that of climb, the D III taking 7 minutes to reach 5,000 feet, compared with the SE 5A's 5 minutes 35 seconds to reach the same height. Notwithstanding, the twin 7.92mm Spandau armed D III's career paralleled that of the Albatros D V in as much as it was to be produced in an up-rated D IIIa form towards the close of 1917. Based on the operational numbers on record for April 1918, the total Pfalz D III and IIIa build must have been around 1,000 machines. (Cowin Collection)

This initial production batch **Pfalz D III** of Lt Lenz, Jasta 22 was delivered in August 1917, when the unit was based at Vivaise. (Cowin Collection)

Pfalz D IIIa, serial 6014/17, photographed sometime after 15 April 1918, as indicated by the machine's Balkankreuse markings. Although the Pfalz fighter equipped a large number of Jastas, it seems it never equipped any one exclusively. (Cowin Collection)

Bottom Each war has its glories and its myths and surely one of the greatest myths of the World War I airwar must be that centred around Anthony Fokker's triplane fighter, the Dr I. Feared by its pilots as being structurally flawed, the Fokker triplane was only built in relatively small numbers, after which it was rapidly replaced by the much superior Fokker D VII. Just how was it then that to this day, the **Fokker Dr I** is thought of as one of the Allies' greatest aerial adversaries? In part, the story involves the 'Red Baron', the publicity machine that surrounded him, as discussed in the frontispiece to this book and Anthony Fokker, who did his utmost to cultivate von Richthofen's favour. The other major part of the story lies with the panic that befell the German Air Ministry in the wake of the Sopwith Triplane's advent in February 1917, a panic, it should be said, that was greater than that which had followed the debut of the Nieuport fighters a year previously. With a climb rate better than that of any current German fighter, coupled to superb agility, the Triplane literally cut a swath through the enemy machines over the Somme. Top priority, urgent requests for proposals went out by telegram from Berlin to industry, Germany must have a counter, it must, therefore, have its own triplane. In fact, no less than twenty different types of German triplane fighter prototypes were to appear over the next twelve months, of which more later. What happened quite early on shows not only how Fokker stole the lead on his competitors, but also casts light on the Richthofen/Fokker relationship. Richthofen first encountered a Sopwith Triplane on 20 April 1917 and was impressed. He soon passed his impressions of the machine and its capabilities to Fokker during one of his frequent visits to the front-line airfields. Armed with this first-hand briefing, Fokker, whose fighters had lost much of their credibility, put his design and engineering team onto the

triplane project right away, thus gaining two months lead on the nearest of his competitors. By July 1917, Fokker had flown and tested his V3 prototype with fully cantilevered wings, that is with no interplane struts, that were added to V4, in the shape of simply 'I' struts, to cure wing vibration. V4 became the first of three pre-production examples, carrying the military designation **F I**. Granted service clearance in mid August 1917, Fokker, himself, accompanied the second and third of these machines to Courtrai, where he personally gave **Manfred von Richthofen** and **Werner Voss** their type checks on F Is, serial 102/17 and 103/17, respectively. Deliveries of the 318 production examples, by this time redesignated Dr I, started in mid-October1917. Unfortunately, for at least

two early recipients of the Dr I, Lt **Heinz Gontermann** of Jasta 15, an Orden Pour Le Merite holder with 39 'kills' and **Lt Pastor** of JG I, their machines broke up in mid-air on 30 and 31 October 1917, the pilot being killed in each case. The problem was a flawed wing requiring the withdrawal of the Dr I pending rectification. Strengthened and returned to service by December 1917, the Dr I was always subsequently viewed with some suspicion by its pilots, the type being relegated to second-line duties as soon as possible as Fokker D VIIs were delivered. Shown below opposite is von Richthofen sitting in his F I, 102/17 and chatting with fellow pilots of his fighter wing, JG I. (Cowin Collection)

was 22 and on 8 April 1917 he was awarded the Pour Le Merite. Voss went on to join Jasta 5, where he added a further 12 "kills" flying against the French, before taking command of Jasta 10 on 31 July 1917. Here, facing the British, Voss added another 14 victories, taking his total tally to 48 before he elected to fly just one more sortie prior to going on leave with his two brothers. Voss had the misfortune to encounter the hand-picked SE 5a pilots of No 56 Squadron, RAF and succumbed to their guns. Voss was the 4th ranking German air ace of the war. He is seen below left standing beside his Albatros D III of Jasta 2, decorated with his personal emblem. (Cowin Collection)

Lt **Werner Voss** stands in front of his Fokker F I (above right), 103/17, which as leader of Jasta 10 he had received on 29 August 1917 and the machine in which he was to die less than a month later, on 23 September 1917. Werner Voss, born 13 April 1897, was not yet eighteen when he enlisted in a Hussars Regiment just prior to the outbreak of World War I. In August 1915, he transferred into flying, initially as an observer, where he survived the Battle of the Somme, launched on 1 July 1916 and a period when the Allies held superiority in the air. Voss left the front in August 1916 to be trained as a pilot, joining Jasta 2 on 21 November 1916, flying Albatros D IIIs. Six days later Voss scored his first 'kill'. By the end of February 1917, Voss's score

With a mechanic ready to swing the propeller and two more in attendance, this **Fokker Dr I** pilot prepares for take-off. Alongside the Dr I is a Pfalz D III of the same Jasta helping illustrate the mixture of types that remained characteristic of German front-line Jastas all the way through to the Armistice. In contrast, the British and French had long since realised the logistical, maintenance and operational benefits of standardising aircraft and engines at squadron level. (Cowin Collection)

Overleaf, top One of the runners-up in the great German triplane fighter requirement saga in the summer of 1917 was this neat-looking **Pfalz Dr I**. First flown in the autumn of 1917, the Pfalz Dr I used a 160hp Siemens-Halske Sh III rotary, giving the

machine an almost incredible top level speed of 125mph at sea level. The twin 7.92mm Spandau armed machine was given two operational evaluations, one in October 1917, followed by a second, conducted by **Manfred von Richthofen**, in December 1917. Richthofen considered the Pfalz to be generally inferior to the Fokker Dr I. Recalling that it was the Bavarians, long time critics of Fokker products and in whose domain Pfalz was based, it would be interesting to know just when they went ahead and ordered a reported ten Pfalz Dr Is to be built. (Cowin Collection)

Below No less than eleven manufacturers produced triplane, single seat fighters in the summer of 1917, including **Albatros**, whose **Dr I** simply married a new triplane wing to an otherwise standard D V airframe. (Cowin Collection)

Three other triplane fighter essays of 1917 were the rotary-powered **Euler Dr I**, (*opposite, top*) the 185hp Austro-Daimler powered **Hansa-Brandenburg L 16** (*inset, right*) and the Korting engined **DFW Dr I** (*main picture, right*). (Cowin Collection)

Quite what Anthony Fokker and his designers were setting out to achieve with this conventionally-tailed, tandem-winged, quintrupriplane monstrosity is anyone's guess. Completed in the autumn of 1917, months after his Dr I, the sole **Fokker V8** is

reported to have only made two brief hops, each time with Fokker at the controls before scrapping. (Cowin Collection)

Below Design of the **Austrian Aviatik**, or **Berg D I** commenced very early in 1917, slightly ahead of Austria's other indigenous fighter, the Phonix D I. During the early stage of its flying career, the Berg D I suffered catastrophic structural wing failure, but once generally 'beefed-up', the machine proved to be both fast, agile and have a good climb, cited as reaching 13,000 feet in 11 minutes 15 seconds. Initially powered by a 185hp Austro-Daimler, these Bergs had top level speed of 113mph at sea level. The speed of later 200hp or 225hp powered aircraft rose to 115mph. Similarly, initial production Bergs carried a single 8mm Schwarzlose, while a second was added to later fighters. Delivered primarily to serve on the Italian Front from the late spring of 1917 onwards, the Berg D I was built in some quantities, involving 4 sub-contractors probably producing more than 300 machines. The fighter shown here was the mount of Austrian air ace, Oblt **Frank Linke-Crawford**, leader of Flik 60. (Cowin Collection)

Right Hptm **Godwin Brumowski** survived the war as Austro-Hungary's leading air ace with a score of 40, according to Austrian sources, or 35 if using Hungarian figures. Incidentally this discrepancy is commonplace, with the Hungarian claims always being lower. Born on 26 July 1889, Brumowski was already a serving field artillery officer at the outbreak of war. He transferred to the army flying service in late 1915, training as an observer. It seems that Brumowski, with the help of squadron colleagues, then taught himself to pilot an aircraft, leading to him being given command of Flik 12 in early 1916. Flik 12 was a mixed unit with both two and single seaters and Brumowski's frustration mounted at the operational doctrine of using the single seaters exclusively as two seater escorts. Seconded to study German air operations on the Western Front during the summer of 1916, Brumowski returned, persuading his seniors to give him leadership of an all fighter unit, Flik 41. Brumowski and his squadron operated on the Italian Front for the rest of the war. Initially equipped with Hansa-Brandenburg D Is, the unit converted to Albatros D IIIs in mid-1917. (Cowin Collection)

Derived from the **Hansa-Brandenburg D I**, the Phonix D I adopted a more conventional interplane strut arrangement and a prominent fin. First flown in mid-1917, the Phonix D I entered service in February 1918, with 150 going to the Austro-Hungarian Army air arm and 40 to the Austro-Hungarian Navy. Not particularly agile, the D I, with its 200hp Hiero, had a top level speed of 112mph at sea level and was said to have a good rate of climb. Armed with twin 8mm Schwarzlose, the proneness of these guns to jamming, along with their inaccessibility in the D I was a point of major criticism. The machine seen here was the 45th of the second 50 production batch. (Cowin Collection)

The single seat **Pfalz D VII** fighter of late 1917 never progressed beyond the prototype stage. Using a 160hp Siemens-Halkske Sh III rotary, this Pfalz machine was one of 23 entrants put forward for the first of three 1918 competitive fighter trials, all at Alderhof, near Berlin, this one being held in late January and early February. (Cowin Collection)

Oblt **Ernst Udet**, seen here standing in front of his Fokker D VII 'Lo' was born on 26 April 1896 and was to become the last commander of Jasta 4, having previously served with Jastas 15, 37 and 11. At the time of the Armistice, Udet was a Pour Le Merite holder, with 62 confirmed victories, which makes him Germany's second highest scoring ace of the war after Baron Manfred von Richthofen. Udet remained prominent in post-war German aviation circles, particularly as an aerobatic pilot and lent his name to an aircraft manufacturer during the 1920s. Along with a number of other former prominent military fliers, Udet rejoined the Luftwaffe in 1935 with the rank of Generaloberst, the equivalent of a four-star general or Air

Chief Marshal. Subsequently blamed for shortfalls in aircraft production, Udet took his own life on 17 November 1941. (Cowin Collection)

Opposite, top Although slower than many of its competitors, the Fokker V 11 prototype's easy handling and reluctance to spin endeared the aircraft to the trials pilots, unanimously adjudging it the overall winner of the first of the 1918 Alderhof fighter

trials. As there was an urgent need for an initial 400 of these single seat fighters, a figure beyond Fokker's ability to meet on time, contracts were placed simultaneously with Fokker and Albatros, with AEG being drawn in later. Given the military designation **Fokker D VII**, the machine was powered initially by a 160hp Mercedes D III, this being soon replaced by the 185hp BMW IIIa. This latter engine pushed the top level speed up by 7mph, to 124mph at sea level and had an even more dramatic effect on the fighter's rate of climb, with the time to reach 3,280 feet dropping to 2.5 minutes from 3.8 minutes for the earlier Mercedes powered examples. Rapid as it was, with first operational deliveries being made in April 1917 to JG 1, the Fokker D VII's passage into service appears to have been essentially trouble-free. Even more significantly, no subsequent fatal flaws, such as those experienced with Fokker's Dr I, were to emerge. At last Anthony Fokker and his chief designer, Reinhold Platz, had produced a real winner that would not only keep the factory full, but would soon come to earn the respect of the all the Allied pilots who encountered it. Armed with the standard twin 7.92mm Spandaus, over 800 examples of the D VII had been delivered to 48 operational Jastas by the start of September 1918. Showing off its well proportioned lines, Fokker D VII, 507/18, seen here, reportedly served with the famed Jasta Boelcke. (Cowin Collection)

Right The youthful Lt **Ulrich Nechel** standing near his Fokker D VII. Nechel, born on 23 January 1898, was still aged only twenty at the time of the Armistice. Despite this, Nechel's confirmed score of 30 'kills', coupled to his leadership qualities had seen him selected to command Jasta 6 during the last months of the war. Prior to this, Nechel had served with Jastas 12 and 19. He was awarded the Pour Le Merite on 8 November 1918. (Cowin Collection)

The compact **Pfalz D VII**I was completed in time for the second of the 1918 fighter competitions and showed sufficient promise to warrant a production contract. Powered by a 160hp Siemens-Halske Sh III rotary, the twin 7.92mm Spandau-armed D VIII had a top level speed of 120mph at sea level. Production was just getting underway at the time of the Armistice, with 40 or so completed. The example seen here was one of 20 that were undergoing operational evaluation at the front. (Cowin Collection)

Lt **Emil Thuy**, as commander of Jasta 28 with his Fokker D VII, 262/18. Thuy had been given Jasta 28 after learning his craft with Jasta 21. A Pour Le Merite holder, Thuy survived the war with a confirmed 32 victories. (Cowin Collection)

Top One of **Albatros's** less notable designs, their **D XII**. The first of the two D XII built used a 180hp Mercedes DIIIa and first flew in March 1918, the second, powered by a 185hp BMW IIIa, following it into the air a month later. Top level speed of the first D XII, seen here, was cited at 115mph at sea level. The second aircraft took part in the third of the 1918 fighter design competitions, held in October. (Cowin Collection)

Inset The second of the two **Albatros D XI** fighters, 2209/18, entered into the second 1918 fighter competition, held in May and June. The pair of small and stubby D XIs were among the 37 competitors entered, the overall winner being Fokker's V 28, precursor to the Fokker D VIII rotary powered, parasol winged monoplane fighter. (Cowin Collection)

Left Thanks to the relatively protracted development of the **LFG Roland D VIb**, only a small number of this 200hp Benz Bz IIIa powered single seater reached the Western Front prior to the Armistice. A handful also found their way to the Navy, where they were used to defend seaplane bases. Armed with twin 7.92mm Spandaus, the D VIb had a top level speed of 124mph at sea level, falling sharply to 113mph at 6,560 feet. (Cowin Collection)

The **Pfalz D XII** was another newcomer to the front in the last months of the war, having been selected for production as a result of its performance in the second of the 1918 Adlershof fighter competitions. At Adlershof, no less than three Pfalz D XII precursors had been entered, each having a different engine, with the 180hp Mercedes DIIIa being chosen to power the production aircraft. Readily distinguishable from the Fokker D VII by it second bay, or set of interplane struts, the twin 7.92mm Spandau armed Pfalz D XII started to enter operational service in September 1918, examples of it going to ten front-line Jastas. Initially seen as second best to the Fokker D VII, the D XII, with its 120mph top level speed at sea level proved slightly faster than the Fokker, which it could also outdive. However, perhaps the most endearing quality possessed by the Pfalz fighter was its ability to withstand a great deal of combat damage and still get its pilot home. With production only just having started up, only 90 to 100 D XIIs are thought to have been completed at the time of the Armistice. (Cowin Collection)

While some of Anthony Fokker's business practices may have been questionalble, the one thing he could never have been criticised about was his attitude towards aircraft development. This manifested itself in a prolific string of prototypes that left most other manufacturers gasping. Although largely overlooked today, these prototypes occasionally bore impressive fruit, as in the case of Fokker's last production fighter of the war, his monoplane D VIII. The story of the D VIII begins early in 1918 with one of those Fokker and Reinhold Platz 'What if?' exercises involving removing the lower wing from the one of the two

Fokker D VII biplane prototypes. This proved a less than ideal solution, so Platz tried it again with the V 26, a lighter, rotary-powered one-off that used the Junkers-devised thick sectioned wing. This one worked, in fact so successfully, that Fokker set all hands to producing the fully militarised E V to be ready for the second of the 1918 Adlershof fighter trials. Here, in the rotary-powered class fly-offs the lightweight **Fokker E V** swept the competition aside, very much as its forebear, the D VII had done a few months previously. However, from this date on, the story of the E V, later D VIII, takes on the more sobering tones of the the Fokker Dr I saga, for hardly had the first E Vs started to

flow to the front in July 1918, than the type had to be withdrawn in August, following a series of fatalities. The problem, it transpired, was a readily remedied one concerning wing glueing practices. Nonetheless, the E V was out of service from the end of July 1918 until cleared in October, robbing the front-line Jastas of a potentially admirable fighter when most needed. Powered by a 110hp Oberursal U II, the newly returned D VIIIs, as they were now known, were only two-thirds the weight of the Fokker D VII, which, coupled to the D VIII's high lift efficent wing, gave the fighter both agility and an admirable rate of climb. Armed with twin 7.92mm Spandaus, the **Fokker D VIII's** top level speed was 115mph at sea level, rising to 127mph at optimum altitude. The time cited to climb to 3,280 feet was 2 minutes. This is one of the initial batch of EVs, 149/18, delivered to JG 1 in July 1918. Around 60 of these machines are reported to have been produced prior to the type's temporary withdrawal, perhaps another 40 may have been completed but not yet delivered at the time of the Armistice. Certainly a number of D VIIIs were among the 143 aircraft that Fokker ensured were removed, along with most of his plant's machine tools, when he fled back to his native Holland. (Cowin Collection)

The **Phonix D III** emerged in mid-1918 in response to fighter pilots' criticism of the Phonix D I and II's excessive degree of stability. What they wanted, above all, was a machine that could be thrown about with ease, not effort. What Phonix did on their D III was to take off the dihedral, or tilting up of the wings from the fore-and-aft centre, and to add a second pair of ailerons to the lower wing. These modifications, along with the use of a 230hp Heiro engine improved both agility and top level speed to 121mph at sea level. Seen here is the prototype D III, production deliveries of which were only beginning to reach the Austro-Hungarian line units at the time of the Armistice. The type, however, did go on to serve with the Swedish forces, who bought 17 in 1919 and built a further 10 locally in 1924. (Cowin Collection)

Bottom Little in the way of hard fact appears to have survived concerning the pair of parasol-winged **LFG Roland D XVIs** of mid-1918, other than that they were powered by the 160hp Siemens-Halske Sh III or 170hp Goebels rotaries. Both were entered for the third of the 1918 fighter trials, held in October. This is the first example, the second machine having a taller fin and rudder. (Cowin Collection)

Top, right Perhaps the best fighter Germany never had in 1918 was the 1917 **Rumpler D I**. With a top level speed of 112mph at 16,400 feet, along with an ability to reach 26,300 feet, the Rumpler D I had an unmatched performance at altitude and could more than hold its own in terms of speed and agility lower down. Rumpler entered two D Is in the second 1918 fighter trial, both reportedly using the 180hp Mercedes DIIIa. Perhaps fortunately for the Allies, the D I appears to have been difficult to build as there is no indication of deliveries being made to the front, even though an order for 50 had been placed immediatedly following the May-June trials. A third D I, equipped with a 185 BMW IIIa took part in the October 1918 fighter trials. The two men seen here with Rumpler D I, 1589/18, at the second Aldershof trials are Ernst Udet on the left and Herr Rumpler himself. (Cowin Collection)

Above Including the sole prototype, first flown in March 1916, **Gotha** built 14 examples of their **G II** three-man bomber. Powered by two 220hpMercedes D IVs, the G II had a top level speed of 91.8mph, a cruising speed of 83.7mph, along with an optimum range of 310 miles. (Cowin Collection)

The sole giant **Zeppelin-Staaken VGO III**, 10/15, went into service with Rf Abt 500 based near Riga in Latvia in 1916, making its first operational sortie on 13 August 1916. Power for the VGO III was provided by six 160hp Mercedes D IIIs, paired to drive the nose-mounted tractor propeller, plus the two outboard pusher propellers. With a wingspan of 42m, or 137.8 feet, the VGO positively meandered along with a top level speed of 75mph. Sadly, the pilot responsible for coaxing the VGO III through her teething troubles, Oblt **Hallen, Baron von Hallerstein** was to be killed exactly three months after taking the VGO III on its first operational mission, while flight testing the lethally tail-heavy Zeppelin-Lindau V.1 fighter. (Cowin Collection)

Below The only **Siemens Schuckert-Werken R V**I, 6/15, was delivered to the giant bomber operating Rf Abt 501, flying out of Vilna on the Eastern Front in late 1916. Powered by three 222hp Benz Bz IVs burried in the fuselage, these drove

two oppositely rotating propellers via a complex web of right-angled power take-offs and transmission drives. A key characteristic of this six-man machine was that its twin boom fuselage was arranged with the booms one on top of the other, rather than being set out side by side in the normal fashion. The top level speed of the R VI was 80.8mph, while its optimum range was 323 miles. (Cowin Collection)

Bottom The Imperial Army Air Service's **Schutte-Lanz SL 13** rides in its shed at Wittmund, near Leipzig. Note the row of buoyancy-countering weights, just visible immediately below the airship's forward section. First flown on 29 October 1916, SL 13 was deemed unfit for active duty and relegated to trials flying. However even this career was short-lived, SL 13 being damaged beyond economic repair on 8 February 1917, when the shed roof, laden with snow, collapsed on the airship. Unlike the Zeppelin dirigibles, which took full advantage of light alloy construction as soon as it became available, Schuute-Lanz clung to wood as their basic material right up until their last two airships, SL 23 and SL 24. (Cowin Collection)

Right, above and below Two interesting views of the three-man **AEG G III** bomber that made its prototype debut in December 1916. Only built in small numbers, the twin 220hp Mercedes D IV powered machine carried a maximum bomb load of 770lb and had a top level speed of 103mph at sea level.

Armed with two flexibly-mounted 7.92mm Parabellums, the G III was delivered to KG I during the spring of 1917. The first image shows a newly arrived, pristine-looking G III being inspected by unit personnel. In the second picture is evidence of the impact of operational experience, with protective mesh guards added to prevent the nose gunner from inadvertently shooting his own propellers or engines. (Cowin Collection)

Bottom First flown in mid-1917, the **Zeppelin-Staaken R VI**, with 18 examples built, was to be by far the most numerous of the giant, long ranged R-planes. Powered either by four 245hp Maybach Mb IVs, or four 260hp Mercedes D IVa engines, mounted back to back in twin nacelles to drive two pusher and two tractor propellers, the R VI's top level speed was 84.4mph, while its normal range with a 2,200lb bomb load was around 550 miles. Delivered to Rf Abt 501, by now transferred to the Western Front, the R VIs sometimes operated alongside their smaller G type brethren in raids against the English mainland and more distant French ports and cities. The Navy operated a sole, float-equipped example of this bomber under the designation Zeppelin-Staaken **Type L**, serialled 1432. (Cowin Collection)

Right, above and below Better known for their single engined reconnaissance and fighter types, the Albatros concern did venture into bomber design, but not with the success associated with their lighter machines. The close-up image shows the sole **Albatros G II** 3-man machine of 1916. This twin 150hp Benz Bz III powered machine led to the generally cleaner and more powerful **Albatros G III** that used two 220hp Benz Bz Iva engines. Capable of carrying up to 660lb of bombs, the G III

had a top level speed of 93.8mph. With the prototype of the G III completed at the end of 1916, only a small number of G IIIs were built and delivered to a section of KG 6 in 1917, the wing, at that time, operating in Macedonia. (Cowin Collection)

Above and below Front and rear aspects of the intriguing sole **Austrian Aviatik G II** completed in July 1917. The brainchild of Prof von Mises, the 3-man bomber had its twin 300hp Austro-Daimlers buried in the fuselage to drive tandem-arranged tractor and pusher propellers mounted inboard between the wings. (Cowin Collection)

Although always overshadowed in the public eye by the Gotha name, the **Friedrichshafen G III** equipped three of the eight German bomber wings at the time of the Armistice. Larger and heavier than the contemporary Gotha G IV, the G III carried a far heavier bomb load and seemed far less susceptible to the landing gear failures that constantly beset the Gothas. With a 3-man crew, the G III was powered by two 260hp Mercedes D IVs and could carry up to 3,300 lb of bombs. Armed with two or three 7.92mm Parabellums, the G III had a top level speed of 87mph at 3,280 feet, along with a duration of 5 hours, imply-ing a tactical radius of action, with full bomb load, of around 140 to 145 miles. Deployed initially in mid-1917, the G III and G IIIa went on to equip KG 1, KG 2 and KG 4 during 1917 and 1918. (Cowin Collection)

Below and bottom These two images lend scale and substance to **Friedrichshafen's G IIIa**. Operationally deployed for the first time during the spring of 1918, the G IIIa used the same engines as the G III, differing only in the adoption of a biplane tail unit. Production of the 345 G III and G IIIa aircraft was shared between the parent company, Hanseatische and Daimler. (Cowin Collection)

Left Hauptmann **Ernst Brandenburg** was aged 34 when he was selected to lead KG 3, 'The England Raiders' by General von Hoeppner in October 1916. For the next five months, Brandenburg's time was fully occupied selecting vital personnel in between visits to the Gotha factory and the myriad other tasks that come with forming a new unit with a new aircraft type. Assembled by March 1917, Brandenburg's KG 3 was fully operational less than two months later. Brandenburg was already a serving infantry officer at the outbreak of war and was injured in action before transferring to the air service as an observer. Gifted with the analytical mind of a chess player, Brandenburg's demonstrated bravery was matched by his administrative skills. Brandenburg's tenure as commander of the operational KG 3 was to prove brief, lasting from his leading their first raid against English-based targets on 25 May 1917, to 19 June 1917, when badly injured in a non-operational flying accident. It was during this time that with Brandenburg again leading them, KG 3 carried out the first aeroplane raid against London, on 13 June 1917. Brandenburg was to survive the war and the fate of his successor, Rudolf Kleine, who, along with others from KG 3 were to lose their lives when the wing's operations were switched from raiding England, to hitting more tactical French targets later in 1917. (Cowin Collection)

The prototype **Gotha G IV** took to the air for the first time during December 1916. Larger than the preceding Gotha G III,

the G IV was powered by two 260hp Mercedes D IVa engines that propelled it along at 87mph at 11,880 feet. With a full 1,100 lb bomb load, the range of the 3-man G IV was 304 miles, extending further as bomb load was reduced and traded for additional fuel. Armed with three 7.92mm Parabellums, one of these was positioned in the aircraft's belly to catch the unwary attacker. Discernibly in the in-flight image of a G IV, shown here, are two bombs being carried under the nose of the machine., positioned to compensate for the extreme tail-heaviness of the G IV. This inherent design flaw led to many G IVs surviving combat only to crash during the attempt to land back at base. In all, production was reported to have totalled 142 machines, 52 built by the parent company, plus 50 by LVG and 40 from Siemens Schuckert. (Cowin Collection)

Below The **Gotha G V** used the same engines as the Gotha G IV, following it into operational service in 1918. Top level speed of the G V was 87mph, while cruising speed was 80.8mph. Range of the G V was quoted as 522 miles, but this figure clearly reflects operations with a reduced bomb load. 120 G Vs are

reported to have been built, plus 25 G Va and 55 G Vb, the latter two variants being equipped with biplane tail units. (Cowin Collection)

Right Hauptmann **Rudolf Kleine** was a 31 year old pilot when chosen to succeed Ernst Brandenburg as commander of KG 3 in late June 1917. Kleine had learned to fly in 1913 and had been a reconnaissance two seater pilot overflying the first battle of the war. While brave, Kleine, as leader of KG 3 was, perhaps, somewhat less effective than his predecessor, being rather more impulsive, particularly in his willingness to fly into adverse weather. Kleine and his crew met their end near Ypern on 12 December 1917, during at attempt to explore the feasibility of daylight bombing. Interestingly, Kleine's selection to command KG 3 was, in itself, unusual, as the vast majority of bomber squadron and wing leaders posts were filled by those who had been observers, rather than pilots, the latter being viewed, as pointed out earlier, more as chauffeurs than leaders within both the bombing and reconnaissance communities. (Cowin Collection)

Too late to take an active part in combat, the 3-man **Gotha G VII** bomber/long range reconnaissance type of mid-1918 (below) had a top level speed of 112mph thanks to its twin 260hp Maybach Mb IVa engines. The G VII's operational ceiling was 19,685 feet, while the range, with bomb load, of 335 miles was clearly capable of significant extension for photo-reconnaissance work. Plans had been put underway to build this type in quantity, with contracts placed with Gotha for 55, plus a further 100 from Aviatik in Leipzig. As it was, only 11 had been completed at the time of the Armistice, three of which found their way into Soviet hands. A developed version, the **Gotha G VIII** (right), similar in all major aspects except for a longer span top wing to further increase climb and improve high altitude handling, had flown prior to war's end. (Cowin Collection)

The Promises In Prospect

Without question, Germany ranked a poor second to France in terms of aircraft development at the start of World War I, as for that matter, did all the other nations, including Britain. What happened during the next four years was of extreme significance. The cash injections made by the major belligerent nations boosted the size of the aircraft and aero-engine building industry enormously, but, perhaps surprisingly, did little to further the technical development of aircraft, although aero-engine development was to see appreciable benefits. Indeed, even the French seem to have made little or no progress in aerodynamics during this period, a charge that could equally be laid against the British, Italians and Russians. At the time of the Armistice on 11 November 1918, one country and one country alone could point to having made any real advances in airframe development.

That country was Germany.

The men that pioneered these German advances were few, but their work was to leave an indelible mark in the annals of aeronautical development. It is to the efforts of men such as Hugo Junkers and later Adolf Rohrbach, who jointly produced the modern cantilevered monoplanes that eventually killed off the biplane in the early 1930s, that we must look for genuine progress. Recognition must also be paid to those such as Claudius Dornier and Oskar Ursinus, whose early use of alloys or other construction methods contributed to the overall advance. It is to these men of vision that this section is dedicated.

Photographed in a Belgium field on 21 January 1919, this all-metal **Junkers D I** was still deemed to be basically airworthy after being abandoned in the open for more than three months. Four Fokker D VIIs on the same site had deteriorated beyond repair. (Peter M. Grosz)

Below The monoplane was far from being a novelty, when the **Junkers J.1** was rolled out in early December 1915 and prepared for its inital test hop on the 12th. What was different about this one, however, went beyond the smooth, fully cantilevered exterior and into the all-metal structure and use of the Junkers-devised, thick sectioned, high lift wing. Built purely as a research machine, the two seat 120hp Mercedes DII powered Junkers J.1 could accommodate a flight test observer. Military interest in the J.1 was quickened by its warlike potential and it was trialled against a Rumpler C I, a machine that was considered the best in its class. Compared with the C I, the Junkers machine was 7mph faster on the level, at 106mph and even faster in a shallow dive. However, being built of steel, the J.1 was heavy and, hence, markedly inferior to the Rumpler biplane in terms of climbing performance, earning the nicknames 'Tin Donkey' and 'Flying Urinal'. As with all of Junkers' early machines dealt with here, the actual design work on the J.1 was led by **Otto Reuter**. It must be noted that this J.1 was the company's designation, whereas the armoured sesquiplane J I was a later machine that carried the firm's designation J.4. (Junkers)

Above About the same time as the Junkers J.1 was making its debut, the **Gotha WD-10** was nearing completion, ready to enter flight trials early in 1916. While not representing such a fundamental advance as the J.1, this **Oskar Ursinus** creation merits more than passing interest for the novel and clever fashion in which the designer minimised the deleterious effects such things as floats would otherwise have on the fighter's overall performance. Thanks to its refined in-flight lines, brought about by the retractable floats, the WD-10, with its 150hp Benz Bz III had a top level speed of 124mph at sea level. At this speed, the German single seat naval fighter could outpace France's finest, in the shape of the Spad VII, first flown in April 1916. Perhaps it was fortunate for the Allies that the WD-10 was destroyed during flight test. The images not only show the aerodynamically cleansing affect of the retractable floats, but also the extremely neat housing of engine and fuselage flanking radiators devised by the Ursinus design team (Cowin Collection)

Right and top right The story of the initial, faltering evolution of the early Junkers metal monoplanes is an enthralling one and was outlined in the author's monogram on the subject in Profile Publications No 187. Suffice it to say here that while Reuter and his team followed Hugo Junker's concept to the letter, their notions of construction engineering owed more to bridge building than aviation practice. They showed a marked reluctance to switch from steel to light alloy, despite the fact that Zeppelin had been using it since 1908, or thereabouts. Perhaps the finest example of this is the **Junkers J.7** experimental single seat fighter first flown in early September 1917. In its initial form, as photographed in flight, the machine was an

aerodynamic and fighter pilot's nightmare, with a radiator towering above the engine, not only creating a huge drag, but totally obscuring forward pilot visibility. At this time, the J.7 also had swivelling wingtips in place of the standard ailerons. The ground-based image shows the same aircraft some 15 months later and looking almost indistinguishable from the prototype D I fighter, many of whose features had been evolved thanks to the J.7. (Junkers and Peter M. Grosz)

Although seemingly out of place in this section, the experimental **Fokker V.26**, precursor to the E V/D VIII, is included to show how **Anthony Fokker** was to benefit aerodynamically from the Junkers company's faltering production engineering practices. During the summer of 1917, it was becoming clear that the much-needed, armoured Junkers J I was suffering a production engineering bottleneck. Under pressure from on

high, Hugo Junkers was forced to amalgamate his aircraft company with that of Fokker's on 20 October 1917. As far as can be determined, Fokker's periodic presence did nothing to unblock the bottleneck, but gave him unrestricted access to Junkers' developmental results, including the thick-sectioned, high lift wing that Fokker incorporated into the V.26 and a number of his other prototypes. Incidentally, this image shows the V.26 with its tail up on a trestle which has not been retouched out of the picture, making the landing gear struts look overly complicated. (Cowin Collection)

Below and right Before and after images showing the prototype **Junkers J.8** two seat close-support fighter and its production derivative, the **Junkers Cl I**. Work on the sole J.8 started in October 1917, aimed at providing a successor to the armoured Junkers J I. As it transpired, the J.8, with its 160hp Mercedes D III, had a top level speed of 116mph and impressed those that flew it at the first of the 1918 fighter trials. Not only did the J.8 lead directly to the Cl I production contract, but its development contributed greatly to solving many of the single seat J.7's ongoing problems. Too late to have any effect in the air war, the 41 Junkers Cl Is completed stood up well, alongside their single seat Junkers D I when operated in the 1919 Baltic War. Powered by a 185hp Benz Bz IIIa, the Cl I had a top level speed of 118mph and a ceiling of 17,000 feet. Armament on later machines comprised two 7.92 Spandaus for the pilot, along with the flexibly-mounted 7.92mm Parabellum in the rear. (Junkers)

No resume of what Germany had up its sleeve in the way of bomber development would be complete without reference to the **Adolf Rohrbach**-designed Zeppelin-Staaken E 4250, dealt with on pages 26 and 27 of the first in this series of books, X-Planes. The other obvious candidate for analysis is the long range **Junkers R I**, seen here. By October 1916, the German Army Air Service was very aware that it had no heavy bombers capable of carrying out daylight raids and sought industry proposals to remedy matters. Junkers put work underway on their R I in January 1917, the design being finalised in March of that year. What Junkers were proposing was a fully cantilevered monoplane with a 5-man crew and powered by four unspecified engines housed transversely within the thick wing's inboard sections. These paired engines supplied power through a combining gearbox to drive the bomber's two propellers. Performance estimates for the R I included a top level speed of 112mph, an operational ceiling of 17,060 feet and a maximum bomb load of 3,305lbs. Where the R I really came into its own was over its ability to carry a 2,200lb load of bombs over a

radius of action of 380 miles. With wind tunnel testing complete and work underway on R 57/17, the first of the two machines ordered, the R I would have given the Allies pause for thought had it gone into service, particularly as even the first generation of lumbering biplane R-planes had proved exceptionally difficult to combat in operational service. (Hugh W. Cowin)

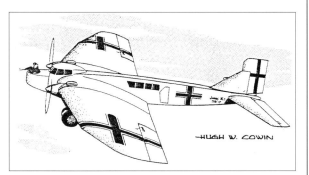

The first of a small number of pre-production **Junkers D I** single seat fighters was completed at the end of April 1918. The short fuselage seen on this aircraft was replaced by a longer one on the 41 production D Is. Powered by a 185hp BMW IIIa, the production examples had a top level speed of 145mph, along with an operational ceiling of 19,700 feet. The interesting thing about the image of a D I after it had suffered a nose-over accident at speed, following a landing gear collapse, is the comparatively light damage sustained. This and other D Is used for service evaluation in the last weeks of the war flew with a non-standard natural metal finish. (Cowin Collection)

AVIATION PIONEERS: GERMAN AND AUSTRIAN AVIATION OF WORLD WAR I